PRAISE FOR

THE
ARROWHEAD:

WINNING THE STORY WAR

"*The ArrowHead* is a modern day masterpiece for all executives who have ever lost a deal and witnessed an opportunity slip away. This easy to read narrative skillfully describes the essential strategies and tactics to win the 'deal' every time. While reading this rich and fun story the reader will learn how simple and easy it is to keep their audience attentive and excited about their message or presentation. Don't grapple in competitive environments. Use your ArrowHead to close the deal; be the leader and driving force behind your institution's message – this book is a must read!"

— *Dirk Bak*

CEO & President, Corporate Facilities Management, Inc.

"Kevan Kjar has brought to *The ArrowHead* many of the key insights that he has so successfully used to help sales professionals around the world thrive in today's fast-changing global business climate. *The ArrowHead* powerfully and inspiringly communicates that we are the creative force of our own destiny –

both personally and professionally. I know his ArrowHead Tools works because I've introduced them to my entire sales, account management and marketing teams. I have seen it enable our double-digit growth."

— Mary Pigatti

VP, Global Sales and Customer Engagement, Fortune 100 Company

"I haven't been so consumed by a book for some time. *The ArrowHead* is a fantastic book that I will refer to it often and make required reading for my management team. I loved the timeless principles taught in *The Arrowhead* as they apply equally to succeeding in business as well as in one's personal life."

— Russ Wilding

CEO, iArchives, Inc.

"The game of business has changed! People today are no longer spending unless they have a well thought out compelling reason; they want something to react to. You must have a powerful and compelling message that resonates and touches the heart of your buyer. Kjar's ArrowHead process takes you beyond having a compelling message to having an emotionally charged story that calls your ideal client to take action. It works because you create and take ownership of your own story, not an outside agency. You and your team together will take responsibility for your own engaging story. *The ArrowHead* will introduce you to this extraordinary path to creating outstanding sales results with your own story and highlights the practical tools needed for persuasive *story-selling,* so you can win your ideal niche in the marketplace."

— Larry Ransom

Author, **Tag You're It!,** *Founder,* **The Synergy Network**

"I was skeptical that a story could tell the story of how to win the story war. I started reading *The ArrowHead* thinking I would read one or two chapters a night. But after the first chapter I couldn't put the book down and kept reading until I finished at 2:00 in the morning. The answer is 'Yes.' *The ArrowHead* hits the bulls eye. Who's on first? Not Kjar and Shaw, they hit this one out of the park. This is a great book."

— *W. E. Pete Peterson*
Co-founder, WordPerfect Corporation

"This is a must-read for sales, marketers and CEOs. Watching a sales and exec team get energized around a message that stands them apart from the competition is watching a company being transformed. Kevan and Kelly have captured it in this book."

— *Janet Eden-Harris*
CMO & EVP Strategy, Market Force

THE

ARROWHEAD

WINNING THE STORY WAR

HOW A SHARP MESSAGE CREATES PURPOSE, PASSION, AND POWER IN SALES AND IN LIFE

KEVAN KJAR | KELLY SHAW

ArrowHead³
PURPOSE • ALIGNMENT • INNOVATIVE DELIVERY

The ArrowHead: Winning the Story War

Published by ArrowHead³ Consulting, a ThreeQuest, LLC company

3167 West Wind Court

Eagle, ID 83616 USA

www.arrowhead3.com

ISBN-10: 1461185092

ISBN-13: 978-1461185093

Printed in USA

DEDICATION

To "A guy named Joe"

CONTENTS

FOREWORD

WINNING THE STORY WAR

A few years ago, I visited with a CEO who told me how his company was losing to an inferior competitor. He then blurted out that they were "losing the story war." That phrase has stuck with me. It is a fitting description of what happens in sales. How else would you describe a sales battle where a company with an inferior product beats a company with a superior product? It is truly a battle on a deal-by-deal basis—and a war when it becomes a pattern. The battle is not over the mere functionality of the product, but more importantly, what the buyer thinks it will mean to him or her. It simply comes down to "he who tells the best story wins."

When I was in college, I had the opportunity to live in the Middle East and see the Arab-Israeli conflict firsthand. Part of the time I spent living among the Arabs and learning of their ways, and another part was spent living among the Jews on a Kibbutz. I realized that both cultures were passionate about many of the same things—their families, their businesses, and their respective faiths. I could see how the rank and file of both groups could get along quite peaceably, but it was a vocal minority that kept this conflict seething after many millennia; they were the ones who fed stories to their "faithful."

In my experience in counseling, I've seen people with a very functional life skillset become debilitated by a story they tell themselves over and over again in their heads. When they finally learn to change the story they tell themselves, they become fully functional and productive members of society.

Winning the story war is much more than just winning a big sales deal. It starts with the purpose of my company, which is to "help people and companies create, tell, and be their best story."

"Story" is analogous to one's "purpose." The impact of helping anyone lock in on his or her chief purpose is the greatest work that can be performed, in my opinion. I first saw this in Viktor Frankl's book *Man's Search for Meaning* and his follow-up work of "Logotherapy," which is based on the premise that the primary motivational force of an individual is to find meaning in life. His findings from his personal experience in the Nazi concentration camps are a fruitful study for any human being.

The ArrowHead is not meant to be a step-by-step manual, but rather, to give the reader a view into the life of a person who lacked clarity in his story, then struggled through and found a solution to help him in his professional and personal life using the ArrowHead Tools. The story is fictional, but is compiled from many years of experiences that I've seen in the lives of others. By pulling them together into this short narrative, it is our hope that the reader will personalize the message for his or her benefit.

Some of the elements of the story have been simplified to keep the story moving; in reality, helping a company create their ArrowHead can take hours or days. It's hard work to craft one's unique purpose. Creating an ArrowHead with a client is a lot like making sausage; the process may not always be pretty, but you love the results when you're done. Helping a client turn over all the stones so they know what their story is, and more importantly, what their story is not, and helping everyone agree to it in the end… this is where I add much of the value to my clients.

I would like to thank many who have helped this work come into being. There are too many mentors to call out by name, but each provided a beautiful string for the weave of *The ArrowHead* tapestry. Because of them, I am able to see further and clearer.

Specific thanks go to my coauthor, Kelly Shaw. Without him, this book would remain several pages of storylines, with few words to glue it all together. Kelly guided this neophyte and helped me be true to my own story. He is a skillful painter and surgeon of words.

Additional thanks go to my clients, who have shared their stories with me and provided the models for the Myleses and Teds in this story.

Many teachers have influenced me throughout my life. Like ancient oracles, they have helped me to see, appreciate and interact with life in a new and exciting way. Special props go to Mr. James Vendetti, my junior high history teach, who gave me my love for all things John Wayne, and demonstrated that nothing beats a great story. Mrs. Higbee, my high school English teacher, who would not let me graduate until I read *East of Eden*. Finally, Mr. Fred Davies, my high school psychology teacher, who first opened my mind to how people think and make decisions.

I would be remiss if I did not mention my family. My late father, Joe, and my ninety-year-old retired schoolteacher mother, Noma. Never has anyone had greater examples, teachers and cheerleaders. My siblings and their spouses have each, in his or her own way, been an immense support to my work as well.

Lastly, my wife, Anita, and our children have each been a "Jake" to me in all senses of the word. Anita and I are so pleased to see them grow, develop, and create their own unique stories and struggle to become their best stories. Anita is my best friend, the yin to my yang; day-by-day, we author our story together, always focused on our ultimate ArrowHead as we fight our story war.

In business success can be measured by numbers, but in life, success can only be measured by relationships and values. I have been blessed with wonderful relationships built on lasting values.

— KEVAN KJAR

CHAPTER 1

THE SHIFT

I t was almost imperceptible, probably less than a two-inch move to the right. Not something that anyone would notice unless he or she was actually looking for the movement. To make matters worse, Myles was already watching for the shift. Why would any VP of sales be focused on a shift when he should be focused on his presentation?

This deal meant everything to Myles. It meant his membership in the Pinnacle Club. It meant making his number and recognition from the senior execs. It meant street cred with his business school buddies, and it meant a buoyant and chirpy wife when he got home. This was a must-win deal, and this presentation was the climax of months of client visits, company brainstorming, all-nighters prepping presentations, missed dates, missed plays, and missed basketball games. Myles knew he had worked too hard and too long on this single moment to not win. That is why the shift to the right by the CEO was what Myles focused on and why he began to worry.

The Spectrum CEO was sitting at the head of the conference table. He had been rather stoic during the presentation, but just as Myles was getting ready to make his closing pitch, he noticed the shift. Maybe it was nothing. Maybe the CEO was tired and wanted to adjust his seating. Maybe he was sore from a morning workout. Maybe one leg was going to sleep. Nope, those couldn't be the reasons, because it was accompanied by a glance at the IT director—not long, but penetrating. The kind of look that says, "I can't believe you made me sit through this presentation." The CEO's quiet, but penetrating glance was the type of high dudgeon that Myles could not overlook.

Immediately, Myles felt the confidence leak from his presentation. He knew the glance and the shift was body language speak he had seen before. It was as if the CEO was waiting for the snap of a football to blow out the opponent. The shift was impatience, and the CEO wanted to move on. Myles knew right then and there that this was bad, very, very bad.

Fear exploded through Myles's brain like a fast-burning fuse, and he fell back on his standard close when the CEO made his shift. "So, are there any questions?" Myles concluded, hoping for a merciful outcome. Myles needed just one quality question that would let him expound on his sales pitch—something to put life back into the room and give Myles some hope that the shift didn't matter.

Myles instinctively felt that "Are there any questions?" was not the best way to bring his sales presentation to a zenith. A weak and spineless wrap-up question would now serve as the capstone, or better yet tombstone, for Myles's months of work. The CEO shook his head no and looked to his IT director with clear body language that said, "This was a waste of my time." While the IT director still had many questions, he knew now was not the time to bring them up. The CEO wanted this meeting to be over, and any further question would only lengthen the CEO's jail sentence and aggravate him even more.

Myles slid his business card across the table and handed out his fifteen-page slide deck (four slides per page), along with a custom-created ROI report with the prospect's logo printed on the cover, in color, with a custom binding, complete with glossy product brochures and white papers.

Myles unplugged the projector and packed up his computer while the customer team sat in awkward silence. He could tell they were holding back their comments until after he left. The VP of finance walked Myles to the door, thanked him for his presentation, and said he would get back with him.

Myles now gone, everyone in the room felt comfortable picking apart the Tangent Technologies product—Myles's product. That's the funny thing about a board meeting with an executive team; once the negative attitude has been germinated, the seed of discontent buds quickly into a full malodorous carrion flower.

The CEO, without even the slightest hesitation barked, "Why should we pay so much for his software program when the other two finalists are so much cheaper? They all look and sound the same!"

Boyd, the IT director replied, "There are a number of reasons why Tangent's product is more expensive. For example, they have a state-of-the-art algorithm synthesis, with a central location for modeling service interfaces and enterprise services for storing their metadata, along with a more open API than the rest."

The CEO frowned with a confused and indignant stare, not fully understanding what his IT director just said. It was clear to the CEO that Boyd was regurgitating some Tangent technical mumbo jumbo that Myles had fed him earlier. It was obvious the CEO did not care for his response.

"Why don't these folks speak English?" the CEO muttered under his breath, not certain whether he was frustrated with Myles or his IT director. "It sounds like we would be paying for a lot of things we don't need," the CEO groused.

Dave, the VP of finance thumbed through Myles's slide deck and piped in, "We may not be comparing apples to apples when we compare the Tangent product to the others. Myles's product is top of the line, full of customized services and support. I really don't think the others offer as much." Dave, trying to simplify Boyd's remarks, crashed and burned; he knew he was walking on eggshells since, as VP of finance, saving dollars was his mantra, not technical explanations. In this case, however, Dave knew that anything less than Myles's software would cost the company millions in the long run. But stockholders tend to only be concerned with the next quarter's profits. A "bird in the hand" is worth everything to a stockholder; in fact, there isn't such a thing as "birds in the bushes" to the stockholder. The CEO understood this principle and knew every quarterly report was the most important quarterly report his company had ever published.

It was too late for Dave's argument; the CEO was already looking at him for support on this issue.

"Dave, does our new tracking software really need 'algorithmic synthetics,' or whatever that thing is called? I am not even sure you know what that means, so how can you possibly know that we need it in this software? In fact, Boyd, the IT guy, is the only one who understands that term in this room. And I have yet to understand anything he explains to us."

It was obvious that Dave was cornered with that question, and Boyd sat sheepishly in the corner. The CEO's fervid tone clearly communicated that he didn't believe they needed that expensive functionality.

Dave knew it wasn't the best time to show the CEO's lack of technical understanding on how the company production software system and revenue approval stream really worked. So Dave conceded to his CEO with, "We can probably get along without that feature; we've done pretty well without it for the last ten years."

"My point exactly," mumbled the CEO with a tone of sanctimony. "But the biggest issue for me is his price. They all look pretty much the same, yet Tangent is twenty-five percent more. People tell me that Tangent is better, but I can't see it. They've got to bring their price in line with the other finalists, or I won't even consider Tangent as a finalist. Dave, follow up on this. Let Tangent know where they stand."

Dave nodded his head in agreement.

The CEO hammered the table with, "Folks, remember our company success is not contingent on our health care–tracking software; our company success is determined by the quality of our product, the speed of delivery, and our responsiveness to our customers' needs. This health care–tracking software is an area where we can save dollars and still focus on our core competencies."

Dave agreed and returned to his office. The rest of the team filed out of the conference room, leaving most of Myles's shiny brochures and white papers on the table to be thrown away by the night cleaning crew.

Myles wasn't in the right frame of mind to return to the office. That would be like the hunter returning to a hungry tribe with no meat. Myles decided his best option was to first stop at Pheidippides Pub. There he could get a drink, drown his sorrows, and catch a bit of the baseball game on the big screen. He thought it ironic that he was stopping at a place that was named after an ancient Greek who ran from Marathon to Athens and then died. He felt a new kinship to Pheidippides.

Myles turned his glass as he was trying to determine what went wrong. He had seen these signs before; he knew the only way to win this deal now was to lowball the deal and hope for recurring subscription revenues at a higher rate later on. The Spectrum CEO seemed to be focused on nothing but price. Just then, his cell phone rang with his new ringtone, "Show me the Money!" Myles recognized the number. It was Dave, Spectrum's VP of finance. *Wow, that was quick,* he thought to himself. Myles straightened his cocktail napkin, took out his gold pen he earned at last year's Pinnacle Club, and answered his phone.

"Hello, this is Myles."

"Myles, Dave here."

Myles could tell Dave was calling from his car, and based on the hour, he was likely on his way home for the weekend.

"Myles, you and I both know the amount of time you and your team have spent on this project, and I wanted to get back to you before the day was out and give you a heads-up on a few issues that you could think about over the weekend."

"Yeah, Dave. How did it wrap up after I left?" Myles asked.

"Well, the biggest issue is your price. We weren't able to see much difference in your product from the other two finalists other than your price. You've got to come down, or we'll have to eliminate your proposal."

"Dave, I am sure you know there is a big difference in the quality of Tangent's product compared to the other guys. I am surprised to hear you say that," Myles said frankly.

"I know, I probably misspoke—our CEO didn't see a big difference in the products other than your price. He wants to focus the company cash assets on core competencies and not on the software; the software appears to be a commodity. Really, this has become a battle of price, and you need to be about twenty-five percent below your current bid to stay alive."

Myles's heart sank. He took another drink to wet his throat. His pricing might be able to come down five percent—maybe. He had already gotten special price concessions to be where he was now.

Myles responded with, "I know our solution is more expensive, but you get so much more. For example—"

Dave interrupted, "Myles, we're only asking you to do what we allow our sales representatives to do sometimes, and that is adjust your pricing downward so we can keep your company in the running for this contract."

"Dave, unfortunately, I don't have that kind of authority to move the price that much. I will need to visit with our president to explore that idea," Myles said, without much conviction.

"Myles, can you give me a call early next week and let me know where your company stands on the pricing? I will then relay the information to our CEO," Dave said. "It doesn't look like we will make a decision on this until we know where everyone's best-and-final price is on their solutions. We hope to make a final decision and award the contract by the end of next week."

"Dave, to be honest, I can't see my company coming off the price twenty-five percent. We have spent months preparing this quote and feel like our price is competitive for what we provide. I might be able to get them to move five percent, but I just don't see our company moving more than that on price," Myles replied.

"Well, you were the last presentation of the three finalists, and we put you last because we thought you would be the best product. It appears, from the comments of our CEO, we are now going to weigh price more than functionally and features since you all look the same. You might want to pass that along to your team." Dave was now silent.

"Dave, can I ask you one last question, " Myles quickly asked.

"Sure," Dave replied.

"Do you think we have the best product?" Myles asked, with just the slightest hesitation.

"To be honest, Myles, perhaps a bit, but I don't think your product is much different than the other two. You each appear to have similar features and functions, and everyone claims to provide a superior product and service. I do believe that you have the best customer service. I guess it comes down to price, and to be honest, we can't justify paying such a high price for some of the extra features you provide—I can't see how we would use them. Myles, you know Tangent is my personal choice, but without the lower price, my vote doesn't count for much."

Myles wanted to go over his feature set again with Dave, but he could tell Dave was anxious to wrap up the call and begin his weekend. "I'll see what I can do, and I'll get back to you Monday or Tuesday."

"Well, do what you can. You know where you need to be to stay in the game." Dave wished Myles a good weekend and then hung up.

Myles stood in the bar stunned. He didn't even get to discuss Tangent's deep bench that was prepared to implement and service his solution. It was as if the meeting had never happened. They must have forgotten marketing's slide deck; they didn't even mention the sample screen shots he had customized for the company. Worst of all, his one shot at closing the CEO personally during the presentation had evaporated like water on a hot sidewalk.

Myles was looking for a silver lining to this dark cloud; at least they didn't give him an outright no. This wasn't the first time he had stood in a bar wondering why every sale wasn't a success. In fact, lately, it felt like he was always a finalist, but seldom the winner.

It seemed to Myles that whenever his company was a finalist, and it came down to two or three other competitors, his close rate was not just declining, it was tanking.

"Always a bridesmaid, never a bride," he said to himself. "Not exactly a great track record for the VP of sales," was his self inflicted verdict.

Myles started to think of the exact words he would use to tell his president of the meeting's outcome when he got back to the office. The thought crossed his mind that maybe he should go straight home and just go back to the office on Saturday morning to collect his weekend paperwork. Then he realized it wouldn't be much different at home; he would have to come up with some explanation for his wife, Heather. She had been planning and hoping that this deal would put Myles over the top so he could make Pinnacle Club, which would be in Paris, France. Heather was a French major in college, and standing on top of the Eiffel Tower at dusk was at the top of her bucket list. Heather had taken a special interest in this year's sales efforts because of Paris. Myles knew the discussion was not going to be pain free.

Myles quickly determined it was easier to face his president than his wife, so he headed back to the office. He put his car in drive and started out of the parking lot, headed to the office. Myles had thirty-five minutes to figure out exactly what to say. He knew the first line out of his mouth had to be, "We are still in the running." It could gradually go downhill from that point, and he could soften the blow with his play-by-play of the events. But then the realization hit; Myles had to first pass the bad news by Cheryl, his boss, who, frankly, worried him more than his president.

Chapter 2

Twenty-five Percent

I t might as well have been free; there was simply no way the company could drop the price twenty-five percent. Myles knew the company had done its best with the pricing for this deal. Despite their best efforts, it seemed like they were still much higher than everyone else in the industry. Every salesperson knows that price is oftentimes the number one factor in a purchase decision. It is natural for a company to want to save money. Myles had always tried to convince the marketing department and executive committee to ride shotgun with the sales team for a day so they would understand the need to be more sensitive to price issues.

Myles's employer, Tangent Technologies, is run by a team of executives who have resumes a mile long. Everyone on the executive team has an impressive list of accolades, MBAs, degrees, and the one resume heavy weight—experience. Unfortunately, their degrees and experience are not at the street level, but mostly technical. It always seems they are behind a desk at headquarters trying to figure out an elaborate technical solution or a pricing model for the presentations given by Myles and his team. Myles was always complaining to his wife that if these "headquarter guys" would come on a sales call with him, they would understand the battle. They would recognize that what they were asking him to do with Spectrum was not realistic. To be 25 or 35 percent more expensive than your nearest competitor is shooting yourself in the foot before you even begin.

Myles walked into his office, unconscious of the world around him. He was lost in his thoughts of how this was all going to play out.

Myles shut his door and fell back into his leather chair with the resolve of a wet noodle. He spun it around to look out the window to see whose car was still there on a Friday night. He was certain that, at any second, he would hear a knock on his door. In fact, he started to count down in his mind—five, four, three, two, one—but, surprisingly, no knock. He glanced at his office phone to see how many messages he had, and just as he was ready to pick up the receiver, the knock at the door came and in walked his boss, Cheryl. It was now time to face a hungry tribe with no meat.

"I am ready for the good news on the presentation," she said as she sat in the chair by his door.

"Well, we are not out of the running yet," he replied.

"What do you mean *yet*?"

Myles shifted in his chair ever so slightly. "They want us to match the other finalists' pricing with a twenty-five percent discount before they make a decision on which solution to purchase."

"We can't come off the price twenty-five percent! Didn't you show them the presentation with everything we offer? Did you show them all the slides we prepared and customized and the sample screen shots? Didn't you explain how much of a superior product we have?" Cheryl asked the obvious, with a machine-gun delivery.

"Of course I did. In fact, I thought it was one of my better presentations, but when I opened it up for questions, the CEO was sending stern looks to everyone, and it was obvious they wanted me out of the room so they could talk. Not a single question was asked, and before I knew it, Dave, the VP of finance, was walking me out the door."

"So, how did they leave it? Are they going to call you, or what?" Cheryl asked.

"They already have. Dave called me on the way back to the office." Myles didn't want to mention his stop at Pheidippides Pub. "I had a chance to talk to him about the presentation and what they thought. He confirmed that this is about one issue, and one issue only—price. One thing he did mention was that we were the last presentation because they felt, going into the final decision, that our product was better than all the others. But, just like I suspected, he said the CEO was really only concerned with one thing, and that was price." Myles didn't include the comment that all the solutions looked the same to them.

"This isn't good news," Cheryl gruffly replied. "We were counting on *your* deal for our second-quarter projections. I'm concerned with always making the finalists, yet rarely getting the bigger, more critical deals. I guess I had better go break the news to Darby and see if he wants to come off the price a little."

"Cheryl," Myles said, "I am pretty confident that we won't get this deal unless we come off the price twenty to twenty-five percent. I don't think I can go back to them with a five percent reduction and hope for any traction."

"Myles, let me talk to Darby; maybe I can get him to come ten percent off the price, and if we do, then you immediately get on the phone to the decision-makers over there and you close this deal. I know we did the homework on our end. They already believe we are the best product, and if you say you pitched it as planned, then we should have a shot at this with a ten percent price reduction."

With the inquisition now over, Cheryl walked out the door. Myles sat in his chair wondering what to do next. It was a lose-lose proposition. If Tangent came off the price 10 percent, then they would expect Myles to close the deal. Even 10 percent was a supreme sacrifice for his company. If they didn't come off the price, Myles couldn't close the deal. So it was quickly obvious to him that this situation was going to end badly. Myles started to feel some panic. If he couldn't close the deal at the current price, and then the company made the ultimate sacrifice of a price reduction, and he still couldn't close the deal...ouch! Not good. Maybe Cheryl would really begin to wonder if Myles was the problem rather than the product, price, or pitch.

Myles knew Cheryl's meeting with the CEO would not be a quick one, and it would not be just about the Spectrum deal. He had worked with Cheryl long enough to know the warning signs and that she and Darby would also be talking about their VP of sales.

Darby, the president and CEO of Tangent Technologies, is a bright industry icon who has enough experience that he is set in his ways. Unfortunately, those ways have seen success, and he is proud of the industry standards the company has established. Darby is more technically adept than he is socially and surrounds himself by a team of similar ilk. He is also a bit of a wunderkind, being the youngest in the "Forty Under Forty" in the state's history, an honor he achieved at age twenty-nine. But, now, years later, watching Darby is like watching a middle-aged man talk about his glory days of high school football. Clinging to his technical glory days, Darby always said, "What got us to this point will get us to the next point."

Knowing he had only taken half his cyanide capsule, Myles headed home to take the other half. He knew his wife had been planning to go to France since Pinnacle Club the previous year. To make matters even worse, Heather had been taking a refresher French course at the community college. It was one night a week, and Myles had agreed to help with the kids that evening so she could go to class. This would test his best sales skills; could Myles frame the pitch to his wife so she understood it wasn't his problem or fault, that it was the company's pricing?

"Twenty-five percent? There is absolutely no way your company is going to reduce the price by twenty-five percent" were the first words out of Heather's mouth. Myles was rather happy to hear she quickly focused on the problem of pricing and not the potential and growing problem with Myles's sales skills.

"To make matters worse, I think the company might go to only ten percent on this deal and then they will expect me to close it, and I am just not confident that will close the deal. It could look really bad for me," Myles replied.

"You mean for *us*—no bonus, no trip, and potentially, no job! That isn't exactly my idea of a happy place." She walked out of the kitchen mumbling something in French.

Myles picked up his briefcase to set it on the table, when the wave of self-doubt hit him. His eyes showed the first signs as he looked at himself in the dining room mirror—no more steely-eyed confidence. Where did the eye of the tiger go? *Everyone is focused on price*, he thought. The client, his boss, the CEO, his wife, and even Myles were all focused on price. What if this wasn't an issue of price, and it was an issue of Myles's skills? He had been in the industry for twenty years; had been to all kinds of marketing and sales seminars, conferences, and training courses; and had read every guru's book on the art of the sale, closing, presentations, and increasing sales production. No matter what it was, Myles probably read it, attended it, and tried it. Now Myles realized that maybe the focus should be on his sales skills and not on the price. It wasn't a comforting thought for Myles, and inside, he began to panic.

Myles spent the rest of the night trying to decide what he could have done differently in his presentation. He wondered if it was his slide deck, the outline he was speaking from, his body position as he stood during the presentation, the suit he was wearing, or even the color of his tie. He was thinking of everything short of his core sales ability. He didn't want to question that; that was too close to home. He couldn't get rid of the dark thoughts, and they just kept circling like sharks in his head.

The weekend was long, and Myles wasn't fun to be around. It was obvious he was distracted, and his mind was preoccupied. That Sunday night, the prospects of what was to come on Monday morning weighed heavily upon him. Heather and the kids gave him his space, but the tension hung like a dense fog in their home.

Monday came and with it the dread of heading back to the office. Myles looked in the mirror and put on his best tie. It wasn't going to be an easy day, but he was pretty sure he was going to have to call Spectrum back, talk to Dave again, and see if he could close the deal with a 5 or 10 percent price reduction.

"Myles, Cheryl would like you to come to her office after you get settled," his admin said with a morning smile as he walked in the office.

Myles set his briefcase down, and with the stride of an injured athlete, he slowly made his way down the hall to the corner office.

"Good morning, Cheryl," he said as he made his way to one of the empty chairs in her office.

"Myles, after you left work on Friday, I pulled some of the product marketing team in, and Darby and I visited with them at length about the price issue with Spectrum. We have decided that we can drop the price nine percent and still make this work for our company. We'll have to scale back on some of the post-implementation services, but we're certain you can help them feel comfortable with that. We need you to go back to the client and let them know our new pricing structure and get a commitment today to go to contracting on this proposal," she said with a smile, which was really more of an expectation grin than a smile.

"I will do my best," Myles said. "I know what they are expecting, and I will have to really push to get them to realize the price isn't the key factor in this decision," he continued. Myles felt like making his case for failure right then and there, but knew that wouldn't look good, so he quickly left her office. The last thing he wanted to hear from Cheryl was how sure she was that he could close the account. The reduction in services wasn't something he was expecting, but he figured it just another straw on the camel's back, another nail in the coffin. He didn't want to hear Cheryl give him specific ideas on just what to say and how to say it. *How would someone so tied to the office know how to present to a buyer?*

What bothered Myles the most was that they wouldn't go to 10 percent. Ten percent sounded so much better than 9 percent, and it felt like they wanted to make a point that they weren't willing to take the full leap to a double-digit discount.

Product marketing never understands the client, Myles thought to himself. Myles knew they devised great logos, presentations, and advertising and that they created enough slides to break the legs of an elephant, but they just didn't understand what it was like to go one-on-one with the client. Myles wondered if he should make the call to Spectrum then or put it off until later in the afternoon. Myles thought about it and figured that making the call at that time would only make it look like Tangent was too quick to reduce their price. Procrastination felt good in this case, and he thought it best to put off the call until after lunch.

Myles skipped lunch, not feeling hungry. He knew he had to get in front of the client again, face to face. He couldn't just call them over the phone with the news of a 9 percent discount. He would have absolutely no chance over the phone. It seemed to make more sense to be in front of the client so he could read their body language as he shared the news about the 9 percent price cut.

Myles dialed Dave's cell, and there was a terse, "This is Dave." Myles responded with, "Dave, this is Myles, I have some pretty good news. Mind if I drop by about three and I can share it with you? It has to do with a movement in our pricing."

"Three works for me. I will have Boyd sit in since he and I will be the two that discuss this with the CEO and make the final decision," he replied.

"Sounds great, I will see you then," Myles said, and with that, he knew he had to produce a bird in the hand. Myles was glad he used the phrase "pretty good news." He felt that it would hint to them that Tangent wasn't going to go all the way to the 25 percent discount.

This contract was more than a big deal. This contract was over $2 million and a 9 percent discount was over $180,000 less in revenue. It was a significant amount of money for both Tangent Technologies and Myles's client. At 3:00 sharp, Myles stepped off the elevator and went to Dave's admin and asked if Dave was available for their appointment. Without hesitation, she showed him into his office. Boyd and Dave were already there, and they both stood to greet Myles.

They chatted for only a moment before Dave said, "So, Myles, tell us the good news. We are anxious to make this decision and move ahead."

"Well, after working the numbers over and over, we believe we can come off our price nine percent. We know that with this competitive price, as well as our superior product and service, Spectrum will be able to," Myles said.

Boyd immediately leaned over to Dave and said, "That won't fly at all with the team. We'll have to go with someone else."

Dave was so stunned at the bluntness of Boyd's comment he didn't finish his sentence. Dave looked directly at Myles and said, "Myles, thank you for your efforts and work. I know this is a big account for you, and for your company, and I also know that you have spent many days working on this project with our various teams. Unfortunately, we will need to select another vendor for this project. We really needed you to come in with at least a twenty percent discount to even consider using your company for this contract. Would you please pass along my apologies to your team? Thank you for your professionalism, and we hope we have an opportunity to work together in the future." Dave stood to shake Myles's hand.

Myles didn't move. He wanted further conversation, and he was preparing to defend his product and price. But just as quickly as he thought of his next line in the sales battle, he knew, in the end, his company would never come off the price 20 percent. Any battle of sales words, benefits, and features would only antagonize Dave and Boyd and probably ruin his team's chance at catching any birds in the bush in the coming months. Myles endured the professional pleasantries and was out the door.

Less than ten minutes had gone by, and it was once again a situation of a bridesmaid, not the bride; a finalist, but not the winner; close, but no cigar. Myles's frustration started to increase. As he turned the corner, he heard his name called. "Myles, can you come in here before you leave?"

Myles was slightly confused by where the voice had come from, and as he turned, he saw the CEO standing in his doorway motioning him into his office. Myles immediately thought this was his chance; finally, he could sit down with the CEO and show him why his product would be their best choice.

"Myles, let me ask you a question," the CEO said with conviction. "Do you think I understand this software and how it works and what it means to my company?"

Myles thought for a moment on how to answer that question. If he was honest, he might offend the CEO by telling him he didn't understand technology. If he lied, Myles wouldn't have much of a case to continue to pitch his product. "Sir, I believe you know what is best for your company," Myles replied safely.

"You didn't answer my question. Try again" was the CEO's reply.

Myles was trapped, and he knew it. He had no way out, and the best answer was the honest answer. "Sir, I believe only Boyd knows which is the best software and what will work best for your company."

"Exactly, Myles, and you did nothing in your presentation to change my opinion, understanding, or desire for your product. That is why it has come down to price," the CEO said, and he immediately stood to shake Myles hand. "Myles, thank you for your time, and tell your team good luck in the future."

Myles stood, with a complete look of shock on his face, wondering if he had just been slammed with an insult or given an explanation of why he lost. With a mild case of bewilderment, he shook the CEO's hand and proceeded down the hall again.

During the long ride back to the office, Myles couldn't get the CEO's comment out of his head: "You did nothing in your presentation to change my opinion, understanding, or desire for your product. That is why it has come down to price."

CHAPTER 3

YOUR THUMB IS BLOCKING THE SUN

I t was standard practice at Tangent Technologies to have a Tuesday-morning review of all sales presentations for the previous week. The review was conducted with the full sales team, and it didn't matter if it was the newest sales guy or the VP of sales, every deal was picked apart like an autopsy in a murder investigation. Cheryl, in a king-like fashion, always sat at the head of the conference table with her requisite yellow notepad. Cheryl is a note-taker, but no one ever knew why she took so many notes, since everything that was covered was generally on the agenda. There was always an agenda and pipeline prepared with the status on each client and the updates from each salesperson from the previous week.

Tuesday hadn't started real well for Myles. Heather's French class took place on Tuesday nights, and the night before, Myles had to break the final news to her that France was more like Mars at that point. The cold breeze from Heather carried over to the morning, and Myles arrived at work with an edge of an attitude.

Myles sat down and took a quick look through the emails to prepare for the meeting. As VP of sales, he was responsible for all salespeople in the company. They had twelve salespeople who each covered a geographic area. Cheryl was the executive VP, and part of her responsibility was the sales department. Sales wasn't her only responsibility; she also had the unwanted stepchild of marketing. No doubt marketing referred to sales as the unwanted stepchild as well; there just seemed to be permanent tension between sales and marketing, an ugly sibling rivalry.

"Good morning, everyone, we will start today with Myles," Cheryl launched.

That was sudden and certainly not typical. Cheryl usually started the meeting, but she often turned it over to Myles, and he would work through the salespeople based on what was most important. This was obviously a direct shot at Myles to get the bad news on the table. It wasn't a surprise to anyone since the news had made its way through the company like feathers in the wind; however, this was like pouring lemon juice into a paper cut. Cheryl had intended to point out the failure of Myles in not converting a steep discount into a contract, and she wasted no time by making Myles go first. It wasn't without notice; as soon as Cheryl made the request, every head shot straight at Myles for his reaction.

"Good morning," he said coolly with aplomb, "as you probably know, the contract for Spectrum will not happen. We lost the bid, and they have opted to go with a cheaper competitor. We all did an excellent job on the presentation; I followed all the slides prepared by marketing, covered all the features, and I believe the IT and finance heads were on our side. But, in the end, pricing was the only factor they focused on, and as usual, we were priced significantly higher than our competition." Myles made sure he pointed out that marketing developed the presentation, and he also pointed out that price was the issue. He didn't want anyone to focus on anything but price, certainly not his sales skills.

"Myles, you are aware we dropped our price for this contract more than any other contract we have ever created a proposal for?" Cheryl quickly reacted.

"I am aware of that, but what am I supposed to do when the only issue they focus on is price, and we are almost four hundred thousand dollars above our next competitor?" Myles felt some comfort in turning the problem back to the group for discussion, and hopefully, Cheryl would recognize he was not the only person struggling with the pricing issue.

Jeff piped in from the end of the table. "Price is always an issue with every presentation I give. It's almost like we're asking our customers to focus on price because we spend so much time defending our high price."

"I believe we are only selling our superior features and benefits when we spend time explaining our price," Cheryl replied.

"True, but marketing always provides presentations that look like we are really trying to defend our pricing, and we are doing it by providing a laundry list of features, functions, and benefits. One person actually said, 'Take away thirty percent of all those features that I don't need so you can lower your price thirty percent,'" Jeff argued back.

"How can marketing expect us to sell something that makes people choke the minute they hear our price? Myles did exactly what every one of us does in every presentation—we follow what marketing provides us, and we end up defending our product on price. Maybe marketing should come on our sales calls so they can see what happens," Hina piped in.

Hina is the renegade of the company sales team. She is a short woman with dark hair and dark eyes, and she is always trying to prove she knows the best way and everyone else needs to get on board with her ideas. Fortunately for Hina, just enough of her ideas work, which keeps her on the sales team.

Myles couldn't believe what was happening. He obviously opened Pandora's box, and Cheryl was taken aback by the quick and aggressive response. Myles didn't even have to worry about the next blow because his team had just sent Cheryl a swift uppercut.

Then, in a calm voice, Don, the oldest and generally quietest member of the team asked, "Cheryl, can you explain to us why our pricing is always higher than our competitors?"

"Huh, let's see, without a long explanation on pricing analysis, it is because we have a better product and better service," she replied in a patronizing manner.

"Quality in our industry is a given; everyone expects it. You can't prove the quality of software because you don't have anything to touch or feel or even see. When I go to the Mercedes dealership, I can see the quality, I can feel the quality when I sit in the car, and I can even *smell* the quality. You can't do that with software. I'm not sure quality should justify the higher price; it can't be perceived based on the slide decks that marketing has been giving us, either," Don said. He just said more than he had in the last four meetings combined.

"You make a good point, but I don't think we are going to change our company's entire pricing model because the sales team feels we are priced too high. Salespeople always want us to lower the price so they can sell more. You are compensated on sales, and of course you want us to lower the price. That doesn't mean it is a good business decision to lower the price," Cheryl defensively replied.

"You might be right," Don said. "Cheryl, do me a favor; come over here by the window." Don stood to walk over to the window, and Cheryl followed him. Don continued, "Cover your left eye with your hand. Can you still see the sun with your right eye?" No one in the room could believe what was happening. Of all people, Don was the last one to take a stand and express himself like this. Everyone looked at Cheryl to see if she was going do it. She didn't even hesitate; she stood next to Don and closed her left eye.

"Of course I can see the sun with my right eye," she said.

"Now put your right thumb in front of your right eye. Can you still see the sun?" Don asked.

"No, my thumb is blocking the sun."

"Well, you just experienced exactly what our customers are experiencing. The presentations are so dense in order to justify our higher price that they can't see the real value of our product. It is blocking everything else we try to tell them. It is that simple." Don walked back to his chair and quietly sat down.

Cheryl stood for just a moment at the window looking out at the view, and then she walked back to her chair, took her yellow notepad, and made a few quick notes while everyone in the room was completely silent. Myles sat in shock. He didn't know whether he should make another comment about Spectrum or if he should just sit quietly and let Cheryl continue to run the meeting. There was an obvious silence—identical to the one Myles felt after he asked the final question in his presentation at Spectrum.

"I have made note of your comments. This meeting is now over. You can all get back to your other work; Myles, I'd like you to stay. We will defer all other sales updates until next week's meeting." Cheryl sat quietly in her chair while everyone silently left the room. The door finally shut.

"Myles, you have to get your sales team under control. Marketing isn't the reason your team is struggling to make their numbers. This is about sales and not about marketing or price. You have to sell what we have, and you have to sell what we have at the price you are given. You better figure out the solution, and you better figure it out quickly," Cheryl said with a stern look on her face. Cheryl was stocky with masculine features, and her direct nature made almost everyone on the sales team cower in her presence, but today's early dismissal struck a new level of fear in the team as they left.

Undeterred, Myles replied, "Listen, Cheryl, as I was leaving Spectrum, the CEO of the company called me into his office, and after asking me a tough question about his understanding of our product, he was very blunt about our presentation. He said, 'You did nothing in your presentation to change my opinion, understanding, or desire for your product. That is why it has come down to price.' I've thought a lot about that comment. I believe he was right. I also think Don made you think with the whole thumb thing. We should take a hard look at the issues. From our customers' point of view, most of the products do precisely the same thing. Just like in a hundred-yard dash, all the runners run pretty much the same speed, but then the winner wins by two-hundredths of a second because he's just slightly faster. We just have to distinguish ourselves by two one-hundredths of second over our competitors. Putting so much product info out there, we overwhelm our buyer, and we look like everyone else. This forces our buyers to focus on price, and this is slowing us down."

Cheryl stood in silence by the window for a minute as she was trying to determine if she should agree, back down, or push harder on the sales department. "Your team has certainly made its point today. I will take it under advisement, but don't get me wrong, it doesn't mean I am taking the heat off your team. The temperature is going to be turned up, and you, above everyone else, are going to feel the heat rise." Without even waiting for a response, Cheryl turned to walk out the door. It was obvious that she meant what she said.

Myles could feel the adrenaline bubbling in his body. It was a small skirmish, but it was a skirmish nonetheless, and his team had boldly expressed their frustrations. Myles recognized he was the one who would take most of the heat for the sales department. If someone was going to pay the price, it was Myles. He couldn't decide if he was happy now that the first salvo had been shot at marketing by his team and that the group's feelings were out on the table.

Myles strolled back to his office, hoping someone on his sales team would step out of his or her office and commiserate about what had just happened in the meeting room. But no one left his or her office. They all acted busy or occupied as he walked by.

Myles's admin handed him a few notes as he passed her desk and said, "You probably have four or five voice messages that I forwarded to your phone."

"Anything fun?" Myles seemed to beg.

"One guy asked for 'Myles-in-Motion,'"

Myles couldn't help but smile. He hadn't heard from Ted since Ted landed an entry-level sales job with AirTrek Technologies many years back. In fact, Myles had even given Ted a great reference for that job. That was so many years ago, Myles could barely remember when it was. Myles smiled as he remembered when he and Ted were college roommates. They both majored in communications, and Ted was always just a little shy when it came to meeting girls, while Myles was warm and outgoing.

One night, Ted hit Myles up on how to work a room at a dance. Myles considered himself the Yoda-master of women. Myles agreed to help Ted with his problem. At the next dance, Myles went to work and, with an overabundance of confidence, found himself going from girl to girl to girl, being rejected by each and every one. Ted laughed and called him "Myles-in-Motion," and the name stuck.

Just then, Myles's admin broke his concentration and said, "He sure seemed like a nice guy."

Myles stepped into his office, picked up the phone, and listened to his messages. Sure enough, the third message was Ted.

"Myles-in-Motion, are you still being rejected by all the girls? This is Ted. It has been way too many years since we talked. I happen to be in your town helping my local team on an important sales presentation, and my afternoon is free. I thought I would call and see if you are available for a late lunch. Give me a call back on my cell, 218-555-2332. Hope to hear from you."

Myles immediately looked at his watch, it was 12:15—plenty of time to still catch Ted and have lunch. He picked up the phone and dialed Ted's cell.

"Ted, this is Myles, great to hear from you. How are you? What are you doing in town?" Myles said with enthusiasm when Ted picked up the phone.

"Myles-in-Motion, it's great to hear your voice! I am in town, staying at the Aviara Hotel, and just wondered if you wanted to catch up over a late lunch?" Ted replied.

"I can't think of a better way to improve my day than catching up at lunch and remembering how I taught you to charm the ladies." Myles knew that comment would elicit a reaction.

"Wow, you must be old; your memory is starting to fade quickly. Listen, I have a car and can meet you anywhere you'd like to eat. This lunch is on me, just name the place," Ted replied.

"That is very kind of you. Things must be going well. Why don't we meet at the Bread Spot. It is about halfway between your hotel and my office. I can be there around one thirty. Does that work for you?" Myles asked.

"Perfect, I will see you there."

That was a breath of fresh air for Myles on a day when he needed it the most. The Aviara Hotel was the perennial five-star hotel in town. Myles broke the bank and took Heather there for their tenth anniversary. Anyone who was anyone stayed at The Aviara. *Things MUST be going well for Ted*, Myles mused as he sat back in his chair. After a few minutes of wishing his life were different, Myles retrieved the rest of his messages and quickly handled the immediate emails so he could be out the door and on his way.

CHAPTER 4

THE TRIAD TEST

The Bread Spot is the quintessential business lunch mecca, the apogee of fine dining. It attracts all the C-level executives. Not only is the food top of the line, but the service is excellent also. And as expected, the high price reflects the service. Myles had eaten at the Bread Spot once before with his boss when they were working with an important client.

The restaurant has an air or ambiance about it that sets it apart from other business lunch spots. The owners of the restaurant are known for coming out from the kitchen and mingling with all the important executive patrons. Both of the owners have a real skill in remembering names and faces, and they tend to walk around visiting with everyone and calling them by their first names.

Often, you will see the owners visit with a C-level individual and then ask them if they have tried a new dessert they just added to the menu. With a simple wave of their hands, a complimentary dessert is delivered to the table. You can just see the C-level folks gloating in what they presume to be their importance. They have the owners of the restaurant visit with them, and then they provide free food. That kind of service and personalization has caused the C-level execs to talk among themselves, and before long, the Bread Spot has buzz—the kind of buzz that generates traffic, and the kind of buzz that allows, almost requires, them to charge higher prices.

Myles was thinking about the service, the food, and the price on his way to the Bread Spot. Just then, Myles smacked the steering wheel with his hand. *The Bread Spot is the most expensive place to have lunch, and it is also the busiest place in town. How is that possible?* Myles thought. The Bread Spot is the highest-priced restaurant, yet they have the most customers—a complete slap in the face to Myles innate sales skills. *The Bread Spot is doing exactly what I have been complaining about. They are the highest priced and the most successful. How are they doing exactly what Tangent Technologies isn't able to do?*

The Bread Spot is the most expensive lunch location on this side of town, yet it is always busy. In fact, it has a reputation for being so busy during the lunch rush that you have to call ahead to reserve a table. It is convenient that Myles scheduled a late lunch with Ted. He doubted there would be much of a problem getting a table at that time of day.

As Myles pulled into the parking lot, he noticed there were more cars than he anticipated, and he couldn't help thinking that all the people inside were happily paying for the highest-priced lunch in town. For just a moment, he worried that he and Ted may not be able to get a table without a wait. *Not a problem*, he concluded, *that will just give us more time to catch up on each other's lives.*

Myles stepped inside the Bread Spot and was relieved to see a few tables available. He looked around to see if Ted was already seated and couldn't see him anywhere, so he decided to wait in the waiting area for Ted rather than be seated. Just as Myles sat back in an easy chair, he noticed Ted pull up and step out of the car. Not what he expected. Ted looked great and hadn't seemed to age much. It was obvious that Ted was done with his business meetings because he was dressed in very casual clothes. It looked like he had put on a few pounds that were all muscle. There didn't appear to be much wear and tear on Ted.

Ted stepped in the door and, without hesitation, called out, "Myles-in-Motion, good to see you!"

"Ted, it's great to see you, too," Myles replied.

They extended their hands to shake, but with no thought at all Ted gave him a buddy hug and stepped back to take a look at Myles. "Myles, I am sorry, I may be a little underdressed. I finished my sales meeting today, so I dressed down just a little."

"No worries, it is just great to see you," Myles replied.

"Nice place—a guy on my sales team said this was *the* place for lunch and said it was the best in town," Ted said as he surveyed the happy lunch-goers.

"You gentlemen ready to be seated?" the hostess interrupted and started to walk them to their table.

"Your sales team obviously knows a good place to eat. I am curious, Ted, did your sales guy say why this was the best place to eat lunch?" Myles couldn't help but try to satisfy his earlier thoughts on the success of the restaurant.

"Well, I think he said, 'People assume you are somebody important when you eat there,'" Ted replied.

Myles thought to himself how interesting that comment was. It had nothing to do with the quality of the food or the location—or even the price. It was all about how they felt when they were eating at the restaurant. It was perception. It was an emotional connection.

"So, Myles, tell me, what are you doing with your life?" Ted broke Myles's chain of thought.

"I am VP of sales for Tangent Technologies. Been with the company eight years now, and we are a company struggling to grow and distinguish ourselves in the health care software industry."

"Good for you, and what about the family?" Ted asked.

"Heather is at home with our three kids. I have a teenage boy, a ten-year-old daughter, and a six-year-old daughter. It seems we spend most of our time trying to figure out how to keep our kids out of trouble. For the most part, my girls are succeeding, but we're learning some real parenting lessons with my teenage son." Myles felt like he might have shared too much information and cut his answer short. "So after I landed you that job at your company with my great reference, what happened?" Myles shifted the conversation.

"It's been a great job; I'm really in your debt. I am now the director of sales and have a sales team of about ninety-five people who work nationally and internationally. In fact, our international efforts have just started to pay off. It is a great company, I have a great team, the product is fantastic, and the team is really what makes things happen. That is why I'm in town. I am here with my local sales team to make a pitch to Langford Enterprises. We're in the middle of a big sales proposal with them," Ted replied.

Langford Enterprises owns the city. They are the largest holder of real estate, and they have also ventured into heavy industry businesses. They are an international and a multibillion-dollar business. Myles knew that just getting in the door of Langford Enterprises was hard enough to do, and Ted was working a proposal with them. Myles was more than impressed; he was envious.

"Impressive, I wish I had the same kind of support and success with my sales team and executives. We are really struggling with our product. Our execs believe we are the best product on the market, and they have priced our product right out of competition. I am constantly battling on price," Myles replied.

"Rather than talk all business, you first have to tell me if you kept the 'Myles-in-Motion' nickname these many years after college?" Ted shifted the conversation.

With that, it was obvious that Ted wanted to talk old times, and for the next fifteen minutes, Ted and Myles reminisced about the past. They discussed what had happened to them, and they both enjoyed catching up with each other. It was obvious to Myles that Ted had changed. He was confident, but not arrogant. He was polished, but not stuffy. He was sincerely interested in the conversation and listened intently—none of the traits he had in college. Simply put, Ted was impressive. Myles started to wonder if, in all the years since college, he had developed any noticeable character upgrades that Ted might observe.

Ted had just finished a story about a college prank they had pulled on a roommate when the food arrived. Ted looked at the food in amazement and then looked at Myles and said, "So do you come here often?"

"No, I have been here once before, but it is the place to have lunch if you can afford it and want to rub shoulders with all the C-level executives." Myles hadn't anticipated that question, and he knew it would look like he wasn't in the success crowd if he answered no. It was not like he had to impress Ted, but oddly enough, he noticed he was starting to feel that way. He reminded himself this was just Ted, the guy who couldn't get a date if his life depended on it, so Myles decided to just be honest.

"So what is this about your software being too expensive? It sounds like it is making your job a little harder," Ted ventured back into the business conversation.

"To be honest, Ted, it is tough. In fact, in the last few days, I just lost probably our biggest deal we have ever pitched, and the issue came down to price. My company was eleven percent higher than the next competitor on price, and that was after we came down nine percent. We are just priced out of the market. We have a good product, but the pricing from the beginning is so high we have a tough time competing. We have done OK over the years, but lately, it has been tough, and I am feeling a lot of heat over the lack of success," Myles replied honestly.

Ted listened sympathetically to Myles's predicament, then replied, "We are frequently the highest priced as well, not always, but I would say seventy-five percent of the time we are more expensive than our competitors. But we always make sure to use the Triad Test before we make even the first presentation. We want to insure the buyer understands the high value we can bring to table." Ted finished off the last of his entrée, then continued, "Myles, you know what you should do? You and your wife should come to our beach house as San Juan Capistrano. It is a great place to relax, and our wives could get to know each other. We have plenty of room, and we could spend a great weekend away from work, and our wives could tell stories about us."

Myles was nervous that Ted was trying to wrap up the conversation after he had just given a great business tip on why his company was having so much success. It was obvious that Ted must be doing very well. To have a beach house in San Juan Capistrano isn't cheap. Myles had taken his family there two summers ago and rented a home on the beach for a week for a small fortune. It is a gorgeous place, and while there, they looked around at some of the homes for sale. Even the smallest home for sale on the private strip of beach was in the millions. *How is it possible that Ted could afford such a place?* The thoughts of Ted's success completely distracted Myles, and he had to get Ted back on the topic of the "Triad Test."

"Ted, we would love to do that, but first, tell me about this 'Triad Test,'" Myles pushed the subject.

"It's simple," Ted replied. "The Triad Test is one of four best practices that I require my sales team to master before we start any presentation to a client. We call these best practices the 'ArrowHead Tools,' which I can explain later. But the Triad Test involves three tests for anything that they say, show, demo or give to the buyer. It helps us filter what we say so we don't overload the buyer with meaningless features. The first test is it must be emotional or important to the buyer—from their perspective, not ours. The second test is it must be different from our competitors, and the third test is it must be defensible or credible. You'd be surprised how much info we give our buyers that means nothing to them and how much is just like everyone else's."

Myles thought about the comment that Spectrum's CEO made to him: "You did nothing in your presentation to change my opinion, understanding, or desire for your product."

Ted continued, "It's a lot like a fishing lure." Ted took a paper napkin and drew a shiny lure in the shape of a small fish attached to a three-pronged hook and then asked, "Myles, what portion of this fishing lure is the fish attracted to?"

"The shiny fish shape, I guess," Myles answered.

"How many fish would you catch if all you had was a hook?" Ted asked.

"None," Myles said.

"Well, that's what many sales people do. They are fishing with just hooks. Occasionally, they might get lucky and snag a fish, but the fish is just not attracted to the hook, or in our case, the features and functions of our products. But the smart sales guy knows the fish, and what they like to eat, and where they like to eat, and when. Then he crafts a lure that is specific to that particular buyer; it's all about what's important to that buyer and how their life will be better with the sales guy's product. I tell my team, 'You don't sell, you solve.'" Ted paused, waiting for a response from Myles.

Myles pondered this simple statement: "You don't sell, you solve." He then thought about the fishing lure metaphor. Was he fishing with lures or just hooks? Myles replied, "Well, the lure that the buyer wants is an inexpensive price."

It was apparent to Ted that Myles had become narrowly focused on price. "Myles, when you went to buy a wedding ring for Heather, were you looking for the most inexpensive ring?"

Myles understood where Ted was going. "I was looking for something that would make Heather happy. So what do you mean by 'defensible'?" Myles asked.

"Well, for us, it means can we really defend our product as the best possible solution for the client?" Ted continued. "It's like the hooks on the lure. Imagine fishing with just the shiny part of the lure and no hooks. You won't catch many fish. The fish has to be attracted to the lure, and then it has to be hooked by it. Your sales message is the same way. They first have to been interested in what you have to share; that's the first test, such as the unique benefits you offer. But then they have to be hooked by it, and that's generally your proof points or features and functions that convince them that you're the one they want; that's the second and third test—different and defensible.

"Wow, that is really good. I am impressed. You seem to have done very well in your company, and you are confident in your team," Myles sincerely complimented Ted.

"Myles, it isn't just that; I believe we are really making a difference for our clients. That is why it works."

"So where did you come up with this Triad Test?" asked Myles.

"Years of trial and error, brainstorming with my team, seeking out experts, finding what makes a difference, and fine-tuning our entire team approach to every sales call. It is one of the many tools we use to win our story war." Ted signed the receipt and stood to leave.

Myles was a little confused when Ted mentioned the "story war." What could that possibly mean? It isn't a story war; it is a sales war.

"I will tell you what, Myles, try this for me. Go back to your sales team and determine who has the next presentation, brainstorm with them on the three tests I gave you, and see how it changes what you do and say. Try it just once, and then we can talk again about what happened. I am going to be in and out of town over the next few months while we work with Langford Enterprises for the final presentation." Ted turned to walk to the car.

"Ted, I may want to pick your brain a little more about this Triad Test. When are you back in town?" Myles asked.

"I'm not sure yet. Just give me a call, and we can talk about the beach house and when I will be back in town."

As they walked out to the parking lot, Myles thanked Ted for everything and shook his hand.

"It was wonderful to talk again, Myles. It's always a pleasure to spend time with you. I felt the same way in college, and I still feel the same way." Ted turned and walked confidently to his car.

Myles stood in the parking lot looking at the door to the Bread Spot. *Most expensive spot, yet the most successful,* he thought to himself.

Chapter 5

THE Vista Health

M yles sat at his desk and realized he only had a few hours to handle a full day's work. Lunch with Ted had taken the better part of the afternoon, and now he was short on time. To make matters worse, he was really short on concentration. His mind was focused on the Triad Test. He wanted to brainstorm with his team and see if they could massage the next presentation to incorporate the Triad Test. It simply would have to wait. His phone had been chirping all afternoon with text messages from his team, and his admin had left a number of papers and reports on his desk that needed his immediate attention. He didn't even bother looking at his email.

If anything really bothered Myles, it was paperwork. Not much of the administrative reporting, calculating, budgeting, and paper-pushing seemed to make much of a difference when it came down to sales. Myles was a salesman at heart and not an administrative paper-pusher. He found no joy in making decisions on issues that only seemed to matter to the people who never left the office. Sales, however, was his bread and butter. Put Myles in a sales situation, and the adrenaline started to pump and the competitive spirit kicked in, and for Myles, that was when work became fun and meaningful. Unfortunately for Myles, it had been a long time since he had felt that thrill and excitement of the sale. He felt like a senior baseball player in a batting slump. Myles had sat behind his desk a number of times and wondered if he was getting stale. Recently, Myles felt like he was trying to do today's sales with yesterday's sales methods, and the thrill wasn't there anymore.

By nature, most salespeople are not good at administrative issues. They thrive on the hunt, the kill, and certainly not the permits, policies, and procedures required to hunt and kill.

"Myles," his admin said over the phone intercom, "I am sure one of your messages is from Thomas; he has checked in three times to see when you are going to be available. He really wants to meet with you before the day is over."

"OK, thanks," Myles replied.

Thomas is the youngest member of Myles's sales team. He's a bit formal, evidenced by his preference for "Thomas" rather than "Tom." He is a go-getter, but he wastes a lot of time focusing on the technical issues of a deal and struggles establishing credibility with the key decision-makers in his sales presentation. Technically, Thomas is sharp. He is an anomaly in the sales world, as he has a technical degree in college, but he loves to sell. His technical acumen gives him a leg up when he is talking to the IT guys. Myles took an interest in mentoring Thomas because he felt as though Thomas had been blessed with a number of skills for success and just needed some coaching to fine-tune those skills. Thomas also has a dry, engineering sense of humor that entertains Myles.

Myles stepped out of his office and headed around the corner to Thomas's office.

"Thomas, I hear you are hunting for me," Myles said as he barged into his office.

"Boy, am I glad to see you. Before I call my lead back, I needed to get your advice on how to handle the call," Thomas replied.

"OK, what do you have?" Myles asked, with just the slightest hint of impatience.

"I have been friends with a junior IT guy at Seneca Foods for a while. We play racquetball together about once a month or so just to touch base and see what the other is doing. We knew each other in high school, kept track of each other on LinkedIn, friends on Facebook, and it just so happens we ended up in the same town, so we keep tabs on each other—"

"Thomas, you were needing my advice?" interrupted Myles.

"Oh, yeah. Well, last time I played with him, he mentioned he was interviewing for a position at Vista Health in the IT department. I didn't say much, wondering if he would land the job. Anyway, he landed the job. He called me the other day, and since he knows what I do, he wants to meet and talk about a new software implementation they are considering. I believe he is way down the totem pole on seniority, but I really don't know what position he was hired for; I just know it is in IT. Obviously, since it is Vista Health, it is a huge opportunity." Thomas stopped long enough to let Myles jump in before he gave more details.

"Vista Health? As in *THE* Vista Health?" Myles asked.

Vista Health is one of the largest home health providers on the East Coast. They have offices in almost every major city running up and down coast. They are one of the top-five largest home health providers in the United States, and Myles had been working for two years just to get contact and a relationship established with the VP of technology, but could never break through. Vista was an impenetrable fortress and would be a cherry account for Tangent Technologies. All of Tangent's competitors were working just as hard to show up on Vista Health's radar.

Myles had always assumed they had a customized software system for all of their needs, so it was very interesting to hear they could possibly be shopping for an outside software vendor for an internal need.

"Yep, my friend said he just wanted to meet and talk about what we offer and get some marketing and technical material from me so he could include it in an initial presentation to his boss," Thomas finished.

"This is good; in fact, this is *really* good. I am glad you tracked me down before you returned the call. Go ahead and call him back and set up a lunch. Let him know that you would like to bring me along, and see if he is OK with the three of us meeting for lunch," Myles replied.

Thomas looked grateful and confused at the same time. Myles knew exactly what he was thinking. It is what every salesperson thinks when another salesperson, especially your boss, wants in on a sales meeting.

"Don't worry, it's your account. I believe you would agree this is a larger fish than you can handle, so we will work this one together. Are you OK if we do a sixty/forty split on the commission? You take the sixty percent, and I will work for the forty percent, and we can work this together. Are you OK with that?" Myles asked.

Thomas looked very relieved and said, "No problem, that would be great. I didn't want my inexperience to mess up possibly the biggest account I've ever worked on. I will let you know when I have the day and time for the lunch."

Myles stood to go back to his office and back to work. As he walked through the office, he thought how amazing it was that a single conversation could change his whole outlook on the day. Vista Health was a huge opportunity for the company, and nothing could turn down the heat more than landing such a cherry of an account.

Myles wondered if he should tell Cheryl yet. If he did, she would start to bedevil him constantly on the status of the account. It would simply be easier to wait for the next update meeting.

"Triad Test," Myles said out loud it to himself.

Myles knew immediately that he needed to work through the Triad Test for Vista Health before he did this lunch meeting with Thomas and his friend. If marketing found out, they would want to give the overweight printed marketing material and start working on the same old canned presentations they always created. *It is way too early for any of those types of conflicts with marketing. This is just a lunch meeting to see where Vista Health is in the process and hopefully to find out who all the players are in the decision process,* Myles thought to himself.

Myles spun around and headed back to Thomas's office. He wanted to meet for breakfast with Thomas, away from the office, and discuss the Triad Test to see if he could develop bullet points and ideas on how to include that fundamental principle in the lunch conversation.

"Eleven thirty on Thursday," Thomas said before Myles even sat down.

"You didn't waste any time making the call. That is great news. I will clear my schedule and make that time work. Let's see, that is the day after tomorrow...that should work." Myles paused a few seconds and then continued, "Listen, Thomas, I wonder if you could do me a favor. Can we meet for breakfast tomorrow morning? I want to cover a sales technique I learned from a friend and see if it could help us with this lunch meeting. There is just no way we can get caught watering weeds again. This is Vista Health. We can't let this come down to price again; we are just not going to water those weeds. Does that work for you?" Myles asked.

"Sure thing. When and where?" Thomas asked eagerly.

"Seven a.m. tomorrow at the Pancake House," Myles said as he stood.

"Hey, boss, one other thing—I think they are looking at a accelerated decision process on this software. My buddy told me they are evaluating options and should have it down to three by the end of the month and a decision thirty days after that. That is a pretty quick time line. Makes me wonder why the hurry."

Myles shrugged his shoulders and started for the second time to his office. He looked at his watch and knew he had a problem. His teenage son had a basketball game at 6:00 that evening, and he was supposed to get him to the game forty-five minutes early. How was he going to get it all done in time?

Myles sat at his chair and listened to the first message: "Myles, don't worry, it isn't that bad. I know you've probably already heard from your mom, but it isn't that big of a deal. I will be in the hospital for only a few days, and then I am sure they will let me get out of here and back home. I just wanted to make sure you didn't overreact." The voice was Myles's father. He was Myles's hero. No man had done a better job of raising a family than Myles's father. Panic was his first reaction, and then Myles realized his father sounded pretty strong on the phone. *What could it be? Why is he in the hospital, and most importantly, why didn't I know?* All these thoughts were running through Myles's head as he called his mother's cell phone. Myles's dad refused to use a cell phone. He didn't really know how to operate one, and he said if people wanted to talk to him, they would call the house. He also had big bear-like hands, and the buttons on the phone were too small for his liking.

His mother picked up on the first ring. "Myles, I am sorry, I should have called you before I called Dad's sister, but she kept me on the phone with all her questions. Dad has broken his hip. They say it isn't real serious, just a simple fracture, and he should be OK."

"That is a relief, Mom. I got a message from Dad, and he didn't tell me what he was in the hospital for, and I was really worried," Myles replied.

Myles and his mother visited for about ten minutes, and then she had to go. Myles could tell by her distracted voice and clicks on the phone that many people were trying to reach her on the cell phone. Myles arranged to come to the hospital that night and see his dad. He looked at his watch and knew his son wasn't going to be happy. Myles was going to be late. He stood from his desk and told his admin to handle any other problems. He needed to go and would see her in the morning.

Myles didn't obey many speed limits on the way to pick up his son. Jake was a typical teenage boy. He was trying the limits of his parents' patience, and he wanted to spread his wings. He had a good heart, but he also wanted his parents to know he was growing up. Jake loved basketball and wasn't happy when Myles pulled up ten minutes late.

"Dad, you know I hate being late to my games," Jake said as he plopped into the passenger seat.

"I am sorry, Son, I was on the phone with Grandma. She told me Grandpa is in the hospital. He had an accident at home where he fell and broke his hip. I had to visit with her before I left," Myles replied, knowing that would take the anger away.

"Wow, so is he OK or what?" Jake asked.

"I think he is OK. I am going to drop you off at your game and head over to the hospital to see him. I will have to miss your game and then come back and pick you up after I see Grandpa at the hospital," Myles said.

"No problem, tell Grandpa I will win this game for him. It is a bummer you have to miss another one of my games, Dad," Jake replied, with the slightest bit of contention in his voice.

Myles knew better than to push back, and they just sat quietly until he arrived and dropped Jake off at the gym. Like most hospitals, the room numbers made no sense, and it took a few minutes for Myles to find his way to the correct room. The door was open, and he peered in to see his dad in bed with wires and tubes attached to him. He looked worse than he sounded on the phone.

Myles was surprised to see Heather in the room. But since Heather didn't have to do the Jake drop-off, she must have heard and came straight to the hospital.

"Dad, what happened?" Myles jumped right in without a greeting.

"Oh, I was going down the stairs with a box, and I couldn't see well. I missed a step and went down hard. I knew right away I had hurt something, and fortunately, Mom was there to call for help. It isn't bad; I should be out of here in no time. You didn't need to come down to the hospital," he replied.

Myles stayed and visited a while but could tell that his dad needed some rest, and after a brief visit from the doctor, everyone knew it was time to leave. Myles's dad would probably be able to check out of the hospital in a few days, the doctor said.

As they were walking down the hallway to leave, Myles turned to Heather and said, "So you will never believe who I had lunch with today—Ted."

"Ted, your old college buddy?" Heather replied.

"Yep, it was a great lunch. You are going to have to meet him. I couldn't believe what he has accomplished, and it appears he is doing very well. In fact, he invited us to his private beach house in San Juan Capistrano so our families could meet," Myles gloated.

"Wow, impressive!" Heather leaned back against the elevator wall.

"Not only that, guess who I have a lunch with on Thursday? Vista Health!" Myles gloated again.

"*THE* Vista Health?" Heather replied.

"That's right. My hope is that *THE* Vista Health will be our billet d'avion to Paris." Myles knew just enough French to excite Heather.

CHAPTER 6
THE STORYARC

Thomas was already sitting at the booth at the Pancake House with papers covering the table when Myles arrived. It looked like he had been there a while, because his first cup of coffee was all but gone. Myles was running late because Jake had started in with him before he went off to school about the fact that Myles has missed all of his games. Once again, Myles handled the teenage comment poorly, and before he knew it, the two of them were in a full-blown argument. Myles had looked to Heather for support on the issue, but as usual, she seemed to side with Jake, and then walked out of the kitchen with the two girls to get them to school.

"I have already ordered. The waitress said she would be right back to take your order," Thomas opened the conversation.

"Great, I already know what I want. Thanks for coming this early," Myles replied.

Thomas had a habit of eating more than he should. On a number of occasions, Myles had told Thomas he should taste more and eat less; it would be better for him. Myles figured this wasn't the right time to teach the principle again.

"No problem, so what is this sales technique you want to talk about?" Thomas asked.

"I was visiting with a college pal of mine who is in sales, and he told me about one of their company's four best practices they use in sales and marketing; they call them 'ArrowHead Tools.' The first one is called the 'Triad Test.' I want to brainstorm the principle for our lunch meeting tomorrow and see if we can apply it in that meeting. I really want to see if this works before we battle with marketing on any presentation material," Myles explained.

"Fine with me, so what is the Triad Test?" Thomas asked.

"Well, essentially every sales presentation they make with a potential customer they have three core tests that must apply to the presentation or discussion. First, it must be important or emotional to the buyer. Second, it must make the product different from their competition. Third, it must be defensible or credible. I am wondering if we can come up with some examples of our product and provide a sharper focus for our discussion tomorrow." Myles explained.

"But it's just a lunch meeting," Thomas replied.

"I know, it's like a quote I read from a behavior scientist who said, 'Any communication is an attempt to persuade.' We are still selling our product; we are always selling our product. Every time we meet with someone, every piece of information we exchange, every action with a potential client is a sales presentation. What we discuss tomorrow will likely be what they take back to their team and will form the early ideas of what we can do for them; we might as well make sure we start off on the right foot and use the Triad Test for this lunch meeting. There is no question we don't know much about what they want or why they want to look at our software, but let's brainstorm a few ideas—or maybe the better word is *stories*—we can share that are emotional, differentiating, and defensible," Myles continued. "What do you think some of their issues *might* be?"

"Vista Health reminds me of my first sale here at Tangent. You remember my deal with Spring Lake Health?" Thomas replied.

"Yeah, keep going," Myles continued.

"Well, the first thing that comes to my head about that deal nine months ago was the freedom our solution gave them. Do you remember how the software we provided solved the problem with the caregivers? Before Tangent, they weren't able to verify the quality and quantity of care they were providing in the home, and our software gave them the freedom to focus on their clients because it automated the routine tasks. They called me back about a month after implementation and told me the story of Sue. Sue was a caregiver of an elderly woman named Elizabeth. Sue was so involved in documenting the visit on paper that she rarely got to visit with Elizabeth on a personal basis. After they learned the software and implemented the paperless data and input system, Sue had enough extra time in the home that she started to visit and get to know Elizabeth. Come to find out, Elizabeth was Sue's second cousin, and next thing you know, Elizabeth immediately had all her pictures out of family and friends. It meant the world to Elizabeth. Sue even arranged for a few of their family members to get together. Elizabeth's family cannot say enough good things about Sue's company and Sue! It was pretty amazing," Thomas explained.

"That is perfect," Myles said. "So what happened after they met? Do you know any more of the story?"

"Well, the only other part of the story I know is that the company rep called to tell me the story and how their caregivers don't have to waste all their time on the paperwork, but get to spend more face time with their patients. They were so pleased with the product we delivered that they wanted to pass the story along to me," Thomas added.

"This is perfect; it has all the elements. It is emotional, it makes us different from our competition because of the amount of time we can save caregivers, and it is defensible because it was one of our clients. We can actually prove the time we save the caregiver and the cost savings associated with that time savings. Not only that, we can prove an increase in customer satisfaction. This is perfect." Myles was obviously happy, as the Triad Test came so easily and seemed so simple to apply.

Following breakfast, Myles headed for the office. He was elated about the new approach. Rather than talk features, GPS tracking systems, billing code transfers, and user interfaces, he knew using a story, even with a techy guy, was the right way to connect the client to their product. It would show how it makes a difference. He couldn't wait for the lunch appointment the next day.

As usual, when Myles got back into his car, he had a dozen text and voice messages. He drove to the office, making only a dent in the barrage of messages. Back at his desk, his first thought was that he would ignore the rest of the messages until he was through with the paperwork on his desk. About an hour into working, he knew his plan wouldn't work forever, and he would have to see what disasters awaited him on his phone for the day. He started with the voice messages and started to listen. Usually, Myles would make a note about any important message and then delete all the others even before they were finished. "Voice message triage" is what he called it. Only the most important get served; the others had to wait. About halfway into the messages, he heard Ted's voice. Myles gazed out the window, intently listening to the message.

"Myles, sorry I missed you. I was thinking about our conversation and the Triad Test. There is something else you need to know before you try that on a customer. Give me a call, and we can talk about the StoryArc."

Myles didn't even let the next message start; he picked up the phone and returned Ted's call. It was his direct line, but it still rang into his admin's desk.

"Ted Wright's office, how may I help you?" the receptionist answered.

"Yes, this is Myles Potter; I am returning Ted's call. Is he available?" Myles replied.

"Please hold while I check," she continued.

"Myles, how are you?" Ted answered rather quickly.

"Great, I heard your message and picked up the phone immediately. You can't leave me hanging on a message like that about something called the 'StoryArc' and not expect me to call you right back," Myles continued.

"I am so sorry, I should have shared this with you the other day. Before you go off and start using the Triad Test, you should understand the StoryArc. It is one of our four ArrowHead Tools of our sales team. I learned about it from an industry expert, and we use it every time we go into battle to win our story war."

There it was again—a reference to the "story war." Myles made a mental note that he was going to have to understand what Ted meant by story war.

"The bad news is I am headed out to catch a plane to London for a sales presentation with my European sales team. I don't have time right now to bring you up to speed on the StoryArc. Sorry, pal," Ted said apologetically.

"I am sorry to hear that. We're going to try to use the Triad Test on a lunch meeting we have tomorrow on what looks to be a substantial opportunity. I guess I will have to wait patiently until you are back. I hope you have a great trip," Myles said, with surrender in his voice.

"I'll tell you what, I have to be at the airport early for the international flight, so I am sure I will have some downtime in the airport. I'll throw it in an email and give you the basics of the StoryArc so you can tune your story for tomorrow's meeting. That is the best I can do; I hope it helps," Ted continued.

"Ted, that would be great. I really appreciate your helping me out on this. I hope your trip goes well." Myles hung up the phone and, out of habit, refreshed his email.

Myles settled into a routine of working through the day's reports and message follow-up. He was grateful that Cheryl hadn't been in his office for a while. Myles didn't love Cheryl's style of roaming the sales floor to talk to each of his sales reps and then coming to his office to see if she had information he didn't have. He thought it was her way of letting Myles know that she could do his job.

"Oh crap!" Myles said out loud. He had to get to Thomas and let him know not to tell Cheryl about Vista Health until after they had their first meeting the next day. He didn't want her to pull rank and start mandating what was covered and what material to provide. He was committed to trying this new method and did not want the focus to be features, functions, and price. Myles knew he was losing confidence in the old "tried and true" method. He immediately picked up the phone and buzzed Thomas's office.

"This is Thomas" came the answer.

"Thomas, Myles. I was just thinking that it would probably be a good idea if we didn't spread the word around about this luncheon until after we have a chance to see how it goes. I don't think we want marketing breathing down our neck on this until we can formulate this new game plan," Myles said with some authority to make his point with Thomas.

"I agree." Thomas paused. "Cheryl, come in; it is only Myles on the line," Thomas said into the receiver so that Myles could hear that she had just walked into his office. "Not a problem," Thomas continued, "I'll talk to you later."

Myles hung up with a sigh and knew right away it might have been divine providence that he picked up the phone to talk to Thomas when he did. The last thing he needed was marketing devising their strategies, pricing, and format for all the collateral they would give to Vista Health. In Myles's mind, it was very simple. The best way to make money is to satisfy customers.

Early in his sales career, Myles's dad used to tell him, "Sales is nothing more than solving people's problems." His dad was not a huge proponent of new technology, as he was always pretty simple-minded. He taught Myles early on not to get too caught up on his technology, the real issue wasn't the technology, it was solving problems. Remembering this made the Triad Test feel better and better.

Myles knew that if a customer were connected emotionally to the product, they would find ways to justify the value almost every time. His first sales manager would always say, "People buy on emotion and justify with facts."

Myles remembered one of the basics of selling is to put yourself on the other side of the table and listen to your presentation as though you were the customer. It was time to 'turn the tables.'.

Myles looked at his watch and hit the refresh button again on his email. He knew he had to have the information from Ted in time to work on the story for the lunch meeting with Thomas.

Nothing yet.

"So, Myles, any news I should know about in the sales department today?" Cheryl questioned Myles as she entered his office unannounced.

"Yep, we need fewer reports," Myles sniped and ruffled through some of the reports on his desk.

"I agree." Cheryl sat down as though she was going to be in his office for a while.

"Listen, I was talking to a few of your salespeople, and I think I have some ideas I will pass on to marketing. Marketing has been talking about a new grid-system presentation for benefits and features on the software. I think maybe we should get together and brainstorm on what sales needs with that piece and what marketing can then do with the information," Cheryl explained.

Myles heard the ding of the arriving email just as Cheryl finished her sentence. He glanced at his screen, and sure enough, it was from Ted. The first thought that ran through Myles's mind was how to get rid of Cheryl. The last thing he wanted to do was get bogged down in another meeting with Cheryl about how her team could "help" sales. Myles often referred to Cheryl's team as the "Sales Prevention" team when talking to his wife.

"I am open on Friday for a brainstorming session if you would like to do it then. It would probably be a good idea to do before our next sales meeting," Myles said while looking at his calendar. He would do anything to get her out of his office right then.

"I will run it by everyone and see if we can make that work." Cheryl stood to leave the room.

Before she could even pass through the door, Myles had opened the email from Ted. He immediately understood why it was so long in coming. It has a large file and even had graphics included. Myles adjusted his chair and started to read:

Myles,

My flight was delayed an hour, so I have plenty of time to walk you through the StoryArc. Remember, whenever you are working with a buyer, you have to remember that they believe they are unique and have unique challenges. It is important you work at satisfying those challenges with your unique product or solution.

You've probably heard the phrase, "Facts tell, but stories sell." We know that stories are the most effective form of persuasion, but when was the last time you saw a formula or model to use when telling a sales story? This industry expert I told you about developed what he calls the "StoryArc." Whenever we want to win the story war and get our potential clients connected to us emotionally, we make sure our presentation meets the Triad Test, and the best way to deliver that message is with a simple story that follows the StoryArc model.

The StoryArc is one of the best ways to reach the heart and mind of your buyer. I have included a copy of the StoryArc below:

The StoryArc

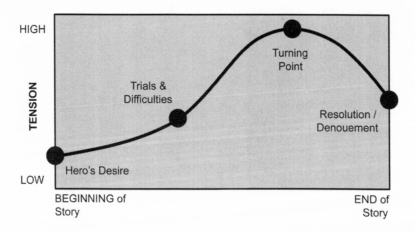

Every story should follow this pattern if you want to win the story war. You'll notice the tension scale on the left; this is the stress and conflict in your story. The bottom is the time line of your story. Your customer needs to feel the tension rise throughout the story and then resolve at the end. This is fundamental to having them connect with you, your product, and their unique challenges.

Make sure your story's hero has a desire, in the form of a problem, that is unrealized and relevant to your buyer. Explain the trials and difficulties they encounter while trying to solve the problem. There must always be a turning point and a resolution. A good example of this is the Wizard of Oz. *It points out all the elements of a successful StoryArc:*

> ***Hero's Desire***—*This includes four pieces:*
>> > ***Hero***—*Dorothy*
>> > ***Inciting Incident***—*Tornado landing her house in Oz*
>> > ***Object of Desire***—*Get back home to Kansas*
>> > ***Problem/Obstacle***—*Wicked Witch of the West*
>
> ***Trials and Difficulties***—*Met Scarecrow, Lion, Tin Man, and Wizard, even liquidated the Wicked Witch, but this didn't get her home*
>
> ***Turning Point***—*Glinda telling her she could click her heels together three times and say, 'There's no place like home'*
>
> ***Resolution/Denouement***—*Back home with Toto and family and a greater appreciation for home*

Keep in mind these stories don't have to be long. You want to use them to connect with your buyer and win the story war. Your whole presentation could be a story, or you might just use a story that will make the point, the emotional connection, and most importantly, the ah-ha moment in your presentation when your customer says, "Exactly, that is what I want."

Now, Myles, I guarantee your competition believes they have the best product, they believe they are the best value for the price they quote, and they believe they want the business more than you do. You have to find ways to differentiate yourself; using the Triad Test and the StoryArc will start you down that path.

Next time we get together, I will have to share our ArrowHead we have in our sales department, and you can't let me forget to also share "Spikes" with you. These are the final two ArrowHead Tools of our sales team. They can really help you focus and win the story war.

Ted

Myles leaned back in his chair and felt like he had just read a textbook on the secrets of successful sales presentations. It made so much sense to him. He was impressed at what Ted had learned since college. Ted was always bright, and although he was a little socially awkward, there was no question that Ted had used all of his talents and skills and refined himself into a successful sales executive. This was great stuff, and Myles knew he was being schooled on the art and science of persuasion.

As Myles was getting ready to hit the reply key to thank Ted, he noticed another email from him. Quickly, he opened the email, and all it said was *Myles, remember you never sell, you solve.* It sounded vaguely familiar.

Myles hit the print key. He knew immediately that the story they were going to use at lunch the next day did not hit all the elements of the StoryArc. His story was a good start, but it needed some work with the help of the StoryArc. He picked up the phone and dialed Thomas.

"Thomas, can you come to my office?" Myles asked, again with some authority.

"Sure, be there in just a minute," Thomas replied.

It hadn't even been a minute, and Thomas walked through the door as if he knew something was important.

"Thomas, I think, before we have lunch tomorrow, we need to make sure the story you mentioned follows the StoryArc." Myles was speaking as though he always knew about the StoryArc.

"I need you to call your contact in the company, ask some detailed questions about Elizabeth and the caregiver, Sue, and see if you can find out the rest of the story."

Thomas looked puzzled, for he thought he had the entire story.

Myles continued, "I am interested in knowing the trials and tribulations they ran across before they used our software and what really happened after they implemented our software. What options were they considering? More importantly, I want to know how it impacted Elizabeth and Sue's lives. What was their 'happy ever after'?" Myles spoke like he was giving orders at a familiar restaurant. Myles also went through the other elements of the StoryArc with Thomas to make certain they had everything.

"Then once you have that information, come back to my office, and I want to hear what you have learned," Myles continued.

"No problem, boss, I will call them right now. Been a while since I spoke with them, but we had a great relationship, and I am sure they will be happy to share." Thomas turned to leave Myles's office.

Myles felt anxious. He hadn't felt this way about a sales call in some time. He decided it would be a good idea to draw out the StoryArc on a piece of paper and then list bullet points of the story at each critical part to make sure all the points were covered and the story flowed appropriately. Unfortunately, he didn't have all the facts and needed to wait on Thomas, but with the help of the StoryArc, he knew what he didn't have. Myles felt like he could get started on what he knew of the story. Right then and there, he made the decision that since it was an IT guy they were meeting with, Myles was going to hand him all the IT techno mumbo jumbo at the very end of the lunch, and then he was going to share the story about the software and nothing else. He wasn't going to get into a detailed conversation on functions, features, and GPS tracking systems. It was all in the handouts. He was going to talk about what the software did for Sue the caregiver and the problem it solved. When the story was over, he would simply ask, "So, what do you think?" and then sit back and listen. He would use this lunch meeting to make sure he knew what their challenges were, what they were hoping to gain, and the options they were considering.

Myles spent the better part of a half hour working on the StoryArc on his whiteboard and trying to answer calls and disturbances in between. As Myles was pondering the StoryArc, Thomas walked back into his office.

"You're not going to believe the rest of the story I just heard. It is such a great example of what our software can do," Thomas said as he sat down.

"Well, fill me in, and don't give me the short version," Myles said.

"OK, so I just spoke with Becky at Spring Lake Health; she was the one who originally told me about Elizabeth and Sue. The caregiver, Sue, is one of their long-term employees. Sue had been caring for the eighty-three-year-old Elizabeth for over a year, and during that time, Sue was always frustrated because she couldn't meet the Elizabeth's needs. Apparently, Elizabeth is a talker and loves to visit. Every time Sue was in the home, she was so involved in filling out forms, tracking time, recording modalities, and juggling paperwork that she felt pressure to be finished and move on to the next patient. They tried other 'paperless' systems, but every report was different, and she still had to enter Elizabeth's information for each and every form. She was always apologizing to Elizabeth. Well, in comes our software. The GPS time tracking, instantaneous head office billing and sync, touchpad tracking, and coding assistant took all the paper grunt work off of Sue's shoulders. Sue was so excited once she learned the program because she could do what she loved to do—spending time making her patients feel better. That is when it happened. She spent some time with Elizabeth and found out they were second cousins. What are the chances? The bond grew, and before you knew it, they had planned a family gathering. The company executives found out and arranged to pay for the gathering and for Elizabeth's transportation to the event. It was a great event. Word of the story spread, but that isn't the greatest part. Three of Elizabeth's sisters were all receiving home health care. They went to the gathering, listened to the whole story about Sue and Elizabeth, went home, cancelled their service, and requested that Sue come and provide the service for them. Needless to say, Becky is thrilled with the software. In fact, she said the CEO was so pleased that he changed

Spring Lake's tagline from 'Integrated Healthcare Network' to 'Caring For You Like Family.' Pretty cool, if you ask me."

Myles was taking notes during the whole story. He knew he had to identify the StoryArc. For the next thirty minutes, he and Thomas analyzed the story, the hero, the inciting incident, the hero's object of desire, their obstacle, the trials and difficulties, the turning point, and the resolution. By the time they were done, they had crafted the StoryArc and felt they were ready for the lunch. Myles broke the news to Thomas that, after the small talk, he planned to just jump into the story and then leave the IT paperwork at the very end so they didn't get wrapped around the technology axel. Thomas agreed, and Myles was comfortable they had a plan.

Myles looked at his watch and knew he had to be out the door. He was going to try to drop by the hospital on his way home to check on his dad. He packed up a briefcase of work he knew he should do that night and headed out the door.

Myles's dad was wise, not necessarily smart in the ways of making money, but wise in more important ways. Myles always regretted that it took him so long to figure out how wise his father was during the growing-up years. It wasn't until he had kids of his own that he started to realize the wisdom of his father.

"Hey, Dad, how are you doing today?" Myles asked.

"Better. They took me off that medicine that made me sick to my stomach, and I am feeling better. In fact, I am telling the nurses I am headed home tomorrow, and they don't seem to be disagreeing with me as much today."

"Dad, this is a great place to get better—why rush it?" Myles asked.

"Son, nothing beats home and your mother's care—nothing." Myles's dad always complimented his wife whenever he could. It was something that Myles really admired about his father.

Myles sat down, and they chatted for about a half hour regarding the day's events, the grandkids, and what projects his father had waiting for him when he got home. Myles stood to leave, knowing he had to get going.

His father recognized the concern in his son's face, and as Myles headed out the door, his father said, "Myles, remember, never sell anything you don't believe in."

Funny how a single line can stick in your head. Myles couldn't get that last line from his father out of his head: "Never sell anything you don't believe in." As Myles rolled that question around in his mind, he thought about his software and the Sue story; it felt good.

CHAPTER 7

THE LUNCH

Thomas introduced Myles to Cho as they sat down for lunch. Instinctively, Myles pulled out a business card. Cho responded and handed a business card to Myles. Myles glanced at the card and immediately noticed the title VP of technology. Myles instantly thought about Thomas's description of Cho's position as "just another IT guy" and smiled.

Myles knew the prior VP of technology because he had spent the last two years trying to establish a relationship with the guy. He didn't know if he should ask what happened to him or just let that issue slide. As the conversation started, he could tell that Thomas was also surprised by the title, and Thomas did the asking for him.

"Cho, you never told me your job was the VP of technology—that's great. Did you replace the outgoing VP or what?" Thomas asked with just the right amount of tact between friends.

"No, my predecessor has been promoted to CTO, the Chief Technology Officer, and I am his replacement. We have about thirty people in the technology department. It was an amazing interview process. It took about four months to complete the process, but it paid off. I am really pleased with the company and my job responsibilities. But it will be a great challenge. In fact, that is why you're here; my number one priority from day one was to put a new caregiver software program in place. My boss has tasked me with the qualifying and technical analysis of our options. Once I have it down to three companies, I believe he, the chief of client service, and the CEO will join me for the final decision," Cho said freely, without much hesitation.

It was obvious that Thomas and Cho were good friends who went back a long way, and they didn't need to beat around the bush much to share information. Myles just listened intently.

Cho continued, "Don't be shocked by this, but they want a decision in thirty days, and then they want full implementation in less than four months. I can't believe the urgency they feel about this. I am sure it has something to do with a recent audit we received from Medicare. I wasn't with the company when it happened, but I know it didn't go well. It has impacted many of our divisions up and down the East Coast."

Myles focused on the comment and realized he needed to know more information about the audit. It was obviously the pain point for their past software decisions. He thought, *This must be the "inciting incident" that Ted spoke about in the StoryArc.*

"That is a pretty fast time line for such an extensive implementation. As you know, it generally takes longer; you must have the whole staff on this project," Myles joined the conversation.

"Well, we are facing some pretty serious issues with our caregivers and customer service, efficiencies, and especially, billing. Originally, we were considering writing the program in-house, until we realized just how extensive and urgent the need was, and now we are looking to bring in an outside software vendor. We want to be able to integrate faster and more reliably with the other company software and services," Cho continued.

Myles decided that since Cho had ventured into their challenges, he would push the subject first and see if he could discover what they were facing. For the next twenty minutes, they discussed Vista Health and what they needed help with and what they believed they did very well. Myles even got Cho to give him a quick version of the audit and why it was such a decision point for the company.

"Here is the bottom line," Cho said, "I was in my office yesterday, and Dayal, the chief of client services, came in and said, 'Find us something that will allow us to focus on care giving and not paperwork.'"

Myles made a mental note of that comment. For years, Myles used a method of getting his clients to visualize the future with Tangent Technologies' software. He called it the "Imagine If" method. It had been so long since he used the method that he had almost forgotten the exact wording he had perfected. But it was the perfect time to resurrect the method.

"Cho, let me ask you something. Imagine if the software you recommended could come in and solve all of those concerns. Imagine if your caregivers could focus on giving care. Imagine if you were the one that identified the proper software, championed the cause, and the outcome of the implementation was fast, reliable, and widely successful. What would that mean for your company and for you?" Myles asked as though he had used the method a thousand times before.

"Well, to be honest, I can't think of anything better, because what my company does is so very important. I really believe in what we do, the care we provide, and the service we render. If that was the outcome, it would be a win-win for everyone involved, but how can that be done?" Cho replied.

"Would you mind, Cho, if I took a moment and shared an experience with you about Sue, another one of our client's caregivers?" Myles transitioned.

It was like magic. Myles preparation with the StoryArc, Sue's challenges, what she tried, the turning point, and the resolution all flowed freely in Myles's story. It felt so natural to him. There was no question that Cho related to the story because it was specific to his industry. Myles wrapped up the story and looked at Cho.

"That is perfect. Sometimes we IT guys get so caught up in code and diagrams that we forget who we are really serving. Your story just described exactly what we are after. Do you know how many Sues we have as customers? Hundreds, if not thousands. Would you mind if I shared your story with Dayal, our chief of client services?" Cho asked.

"Not at all," Myles replied.

Amazing, Myles thought to himself. For a moment, Myles zoned out of the conversation while Thomas and Cho chatted. Myles ruminated about how it was so easy, so different than all the other lunch meetings, and so effective. Cho even wanted to go back and share the story with Dayal. Myles was stoked, but he knew this was just the beginning.

It came time to wrap up their lunch. Myles looked down at the seat next to him and realized all the technical data was in the packet he had prepared.

"Cho, we know you need to be comfortable with all the technology behind our solutions. We have prepared all the technical data, schematics, screen shots, and performance results for you. Here is the package. Look it over and analyze it, as you would like. We would be happy to put you in touch with our technical staff, and you can powwow on all the behind-the-scenes magic of our software. We would love to meet with your CTO and chief of client services whenever you feel it is appropriate. Where would you like to go from here?" Myles asked.

"I have a meeting in a week to review all the solutions and their information. We will know by then who the finalists are and what we are looking at for continued study. I will have one of my lead techs call your technical guys and work through these details in the next few days. I'll work through Thomas, if that is OK, and will let you know where it stands next week," Cho said.

With that, the lunch was over, and they were headed out the door. As Myles and Thomas got in the car, they gave each other a high five.

Thomas looked at Myles and said, "So much for keeping this quiet," with an appropriate level of sarcasm. "They are going to call our tech guys and start asking all kinds of questions. I'll let them know the calls will be coming, and then the word is going to be out. I am sure glad it is you that has to deal with Cheryl, marketing, and all the pricing problems," Thomas said with a smile.

CHAPTER 8

THE ARROWHEAD

"T he bitter and the sweet" is how Myles viewed the lunch. Everything about the lunch meeting was perfectly sweet, and everything about letting Cheryl and the executive team know was going to be downright bitter.

Myles sat in his office chair and knew he had to make the call. Once the word was out, he was going to have two problems on his hands: First, he knew Cheryl would give him some heat about the fact that they had lunch with Vista Health and didn't tell her; second, they were immediately going to go into the analysis paralysis on how to handle the account, collateral material, presentation, and pricing. Not fun. Myles thought to himself just how much of a killjoy Cheryl could be to the sales process.

"Myles, this came for you while you were at lunch." Myles's admin walked into the room and put a wooden box on his desk.

The entire box was stained a deep-mahogany color. It was beautifully handcrafted and delicate in its detail. Myles noticed that the edges of the box had been hand-dovetailed. The hinge on the length of the back of the box had been delicately carved so it was inlaid with precision. The latch on the front of the box was brass, with a small clasp that held the lid firmly closed.

"Who sent the box?" Myles asked his admin.

"Don't know. It just came by delivery service," she replied.

"Hmm, I wasn't expecting anything—and certainly not this. Did the delivery service leave a receipt that said who it was from?" Myles asked as his admin stepped outside his door.

"I'll check," she replied.

Only a few seconds later, she poked her head back in the office and said, "Ted from AirTrek Technologies."

Myles didn't think it was possible that Ted sent this since he was in Europe. Ted must have arranged to have it sent to Myles before he left. There could be no other explanation.

Myles delayed the call to Cheryl; he had to know what was in the box before he tasted the bitter dregs of calling her. He slid the latch, slowly opened the case, and immediately smelled the fragrance of seasoned wood—the same smell you get when walk into a fine furniture store, but not new furniture, fine antique furniture. The box interior was completely lined with velvet that had been fitted around a stainless steel arrowhead. The blades of the arrowhead were razor sharp, and the point was pointed and lethal. Just the look of the arrowhead was intimidating. It was firmly pressed into a fitted position in the center of the box. Just below the arrowhead and next to the latch was a gold plate that had been engraved with the following inscription: *Win the Story War.* Myles noticed the second line that read, "Purpose, Alignment, Innovative Delivery."

As Myles fingered the inscription, he wondered what such a nice gift meant. Why the arrowhead? And why had Ted sent this over? Ted had referred to the "ArrowHead Tools" and told him that he would tell him about that later; maybe now was later.

"Myles, I'm sorry, I just noticed this letter that came with the delivery. It must have been under the box, and when I was back at my desk, I noticed it. It is addressed to you," Myles's admin said and placed the envelope on his desk.

Myles immediately grabbed his letter opener and slid it across the top, unfolded the letter, and began to read:

Dear Myles,

I have always been grateful for how you treated me and mentored me during our college years. I know Myles-in-Motion was always in fun, but I have always been grateful for what you did for me in college, in addition to helping me land my first job with AirTrek Technologies. I hope our recent discussions have been helpful to you.

I give each of my salespeople the following gift when they have completed our ArrowHead training. I know that may not mean a lot to you now, but the ArrowHead Tools I am sharing with you are all included in that training. To be honest, I can't take full responsibility for the tools and the training. They have been developed over the years with the help of an industry guru who I work with. The ArrowHead is the pinnacle of the four ArrowHead Tools. Let me explain.

Inside is an ArrowHead. The ArrowHead represents the core of what we want the buyer to take away from sales engagements. In our story, you might say it is the "moral of the story"—or if it were a Harvard case study, you might call it the "Takeaways." It is the boiled-down sweetness of our presentation, or story, that meets all three elements of the Triad Test.

Myles, imagine every sales presentation is an arrow. What most salespeople do is shoot arrows without arrowheads—arrows of features and functions, all about the seller, with no point on them. It just doesn't stick; they simply bounce off the target. The ArrowHead, on the other hand, is all about the unique benefits to the buyer boiled down to three or four points and told from their perspective so it penetrates and sticks. The ArrowHead provides guidance and context for all the features and functions of the shaft, and the shaft now provides weight so it penetrates.

In a nutshell, the ArrowHead is our product's unique purpose and solution to our buyer. But the ArrowHead can also be the unique purpose of a company, a team, or even a person. That's what makes it so powerful. Purpose is the backbone of any story; it is the hero's mission or journey, which is why it resonates so well with the ArrowHead.

We use this ArrowHead for everything we decide to present or say to a prospect. We also use it in establishing business and personal goals and objectives. Whenever we are preparing for a client engagement, our team ArrowHead and commitment is to:

Win the Story War, and to do this we must:

> *Create our purpose,*

> *Align our team around that purpose,*

> *And have an innovative delivery of that purpose,*

not just the same old slide decks.

The ArrowHead

Win The Story War

Create Our PURPOSE

INNOVATIVE DELIVERY

ALIGN Our Team

These are the critical elements that must be mastered. Now, about this story war— have you ever lost a deal to an inferior product or lost a deal because the prospect thought it was better to wait or do nothing? Or have you ever had a prospect that got into a price debate with you because they couldn't recognize the value your solution provided? Or have you lost your self-confidence because you were focused on your weaknesses rather than your strengths? That's losing the story war.

We have seen it over and over again that people make business decisions based upon emotion, and then they justify those decisions with facts and supporting data. Stories are emotional, they connect with people, and these people then visualize with their minds, internalize with feeling, and create realistic bonds and relationships. Once that is accomplished, they will ensure the facts support the story, and you have won the account. Once they buy your story, they will likely buy your product. That is winning the story war.

I wanted to give this to you in person, but knew you needed it before I returned; you mentioned your company is working hard to get aligned in working toward the same goal. I thought this might help you breathe some life into your team.

Again, thank you for your friendship.

Best of luck,

Ted

Myles's admin broke the silence over the intercom. "Myles, your wife is on line one."

"Myles, I just wanted to remind you that Jake has a game tonight, and you really need to be there." Heather didn't even say hello before she spoke her mind.

"Honey, I might have to work late tonight. We had a great lunch meeting with Vista, but I haven't talked to Cheryl yet, and I am sure she will want to stay late to strategize on this Vista Health deal," Myles seemed to beg.

"Myles, really? Do you think Jake cares about any of your work stuff? He only knows that he is going to go through an entire basketball season and his dad hasn't come to a single game!" With that, Heather hung up. She never hangs up on Myles.

Myles held the receiver in shock. He didn't hear an overabundance of anger in her voice, just your typical disappointment, but not enough to hang up on him. Myles looked around as if he had been caught being hung up on and slowly set the receiver down.

"Myles, Cheryl wants you in her office," his admin interjected again.

Immediately, Myles rolled his eyes and knew the day was getting worse. He wondered how long he could look at the ArrowHead before he had to walk down to her office. He slowly closed the lid and straightened a few reports on his desk. He looked at his clock; it was 3:30. He was still thinking about his wife and the phone call as he stood to leave his office.

"Myles, Barb from the Brickland Community Theatre is on the line," his admin held up the phone, expecting him to take the call.

Myles rolled his eyes again and wondered how much more could go wrong in one day. Myles chaired the fundraising committee for the community theater, and it seemed like they could never get enough of his time. Myles motioned to his admin that now wasn't a good time and started to walk down the hall.

"Myles, she wants to confirm that you are going to chair the monthly meeting tonight at six thirty at the theater," she replied.

"What a bad night," he grumbled under his voice. "Um, tell her I remember, and I will be there." Myles made a mental note that he now had three conflicts for the night: work, his son, and the community theater. Two of the three were not going to be happy with him. It was like watching water being poured into a colander. It doesn't matter how fast the water goes in; there are too many holes, and it drains even faster. *I just can't win*, Myles thought to himself.

Myles rounded the corner and walked into Cheryl's office. "You rang?" he said, with just the slightest hint of impatience and humor in his voice.

"I was visiting with Thomas, and he mentioned you had some news, but I couldn't get the news out of him, so here you are. What's up?" she asked.

Myles was hoping he could do this with a little more preparation than just walking in after being hung up on by his wife and reminded of a meeting he wasn't prepared for with the community theater.

Without even the least hesitation, Myles decided to just be out with it. "Thomas and I met with the VP of technology today at Vista Health. They are shopping for software, and we are in the running."

"Wow! Are you serious? That is huge news! Why didn't I know about this meeting?" Cheryl said, with a hint of tact to drive one crazy.

"Thomas and I actually thought our lunch appointment was with a very junior IT guy, but we came to find out Thomas's friend had landed the VP job. Looks like the old VP of technology has been bumped up to CTO," Myles replied, trying to downplay the lunch.

"So what happened?" Cheryl continued.

"It went well; in fact, we connected really well because I applied a couple new sales techniques called the Triad Test and the StoryArc." Myles decided to come at Cheryl with both barrels loaded.

"What are you talking about?" she said with confusion.

Myles knew he was into it now. You can't just put one toe in the water with Cheryl; you have to get completely wet. She wants the whole story. Myles sat back in his chair and proceeded to give the long version of the meeting, the story, and the fact that they had just handed the technology information to him and never even discussed the features and functions of the product. But Myles knew to hold back on the real information with the StoryArc and the Triad Test. He knew Cheryl would spend more time trying to figure those out, and for now, he thought it best to keep the focus on Vista Health.

Then Myles dropped the bomb: "They failed a recent audit and realize they need a new software solution for their caregivers as soon as possible. They want to narrow this down to three options by the end of the month, have full presentations by the finalists, decide in thirty days, and be fully implemented in four months. They are on a fast track with this decision. I don't know all the reasons why, but it is obvious all the executives are involved, and this will move quickly," Myles said as he relaxed in his chair. He knew he had opened the floodgates, and now it was time to manage the water flow. Relief spread across Myles's face once he knew he now had the information out and could stop dreading telling Cheryl.

"We really need to ramp up for this. Vista would be the largest customer for our company and would really make all of our lives easier if we landed this contract," Cheryl said.

"They said they would contact our tech people this week to check all the bits, bytes, and technical stuff and would have a decision on whether we were qualified to be in the final three by next week," Myles continued.

"We need to meet with marketing, bring Darby up to speed, coordinate with tech to see how much implementation is going to be required, and start doing some pricing models and slides," Cheryl started into her normal routine for getting a client presentation ready and the pricing prepared.

"Cheryl, would you mind if we took a slightly different approach to this opportunity. I have some ideas I would like to use, and I would love a chance to get everyone on board for this. Before we go down that road, I wonder if I can ask a favor. Can you hold on getting everyone involved until tomorrow? I would like one hour of your time to present my ideas. If you don't think they merit value, we can go back to the old method and system of getting ready. Otherwise, just hear me out on a few new ideas for landing Vista." Myles couldn't believe what he was saying. He just committed to presenting the concept of winning the story war. It meant getting the whole company behind the concept of creating a winning story by creating a purpose or ArrowHead, aligning the team, and creating an innovative delivery of that message. He had just barely read the concept and was already committed to staking his career on this idea...It felt good. It felt right.

"It is four o'clock, and I would have everyone stay late to work on this, but I don't think one day will matter. And based on our recent lack of successes, we're probably ready for some new ideas. Ten a.m. in my office tomorrow morning. You have one hour," Cheryl said.

And with that quick and unexpected response, Myles was walking out the door determined.

One of the three conflicts had just solved itself. He wouldn't have to be at the office late; however, he would have a lot of work to do at home and probably late into the night to get ready for what he wanted to present to Cheryl. He would have to deal with Heather and Jake after his community theatre meeting later that night. Myles settled into his chair to finish off the day's work.

CHAPTER 9

BRICKLAND COMMUNITY THEATRE VS. BASKETBALL GAME

B rickland Community Theatre had approached Myles about two years before and asked for his help in fundraising. Myles wasn't anxious to get involved, but his ten-year-old daughter Emily loved the youth drama classes and plays they provided. She dreamed of becoming a Broadway actress after Myles and Heather took her to see Wicked on Broadway. Myles thought his help would be a great way to give back to the community and stay involved with his daughter. What Myles didn't understand was the time commitment. Tough economic times were making it difficult for the stable of donors to keep up with their monetary expenditures. In addition, new donors were very hard to come by. Myles had given sporadic time and commitment to Brickland, but he knew they were disappointed, and more importantly, he knew his daughter was disappointed. Just last month, they announced that the afterschool youth plays would no longer be offered due to a lack of funding.

Myles wondered what to do as he wrapped up the last of the reports he needed to finish for the day. He knew his son and his wife would be very disappointed if he didn't make the basketball game, and he also knew that if he didn't show up to the fundraising meeting, it would be very difficult for the fundraising staff and he wouldn't be keeping his commitments to the theater. It was like choosing between death by starvation or death by dehydration.

No matter which one he selected, he knew Heather would be disappointed. Then it crossed his mind that maybe he should let her choose which commitment he kept. Myles determined that would be his last call before he left the office, and he picked up the phone to dial Heather.

"I wasn't sure you would pick up the phone," Myles said after Heather answered.

"What do you mean?" she replied.

"Well, you hung up on me earlier." Myles paused for effect, but Heather didn't jump in and comment; it was deathly quiet on the other end of the line.

"I have a dilemma tonight, and I thought I would get your advice on what to do," Myles continued.

"Brickland Community Theatre called, and tonight is the fundraising committee meeting I am supposed to chair. We are discussing what donors and programs we can approach to try to keep the afterschool youth workshops open. And as you so pointedly told me earlier, the other option is Jake's basketball game. So since you chewed my head off on our last phone call about missing all of his games, I thought I would call to see which commitment you want me to keep," Myles said, with a slight amount of sarcasm.

"Oh, honey, I am sorry about hanging up on you; I was just very frustrated. And it doesn't look like it is going to get any better, because no matter what you do tonight, there will be a winner and a loser in our family," Heather said in a softer tone. She was always good about forgiveness and moving on.

"Yep, so what should I do?" Myles pressed.

There was a noticeable pause on the phone as Heather thought through the options.

"Jake isn't going to be happy, and he has heard every excuse there is about work and your commitments. This will just be another excuse, but you better go to the Brickland Community Theatre meeting," Heather answered.

"Will you try to explain to Jake why I couldn't make the game, and maybe you can soften him up a little?" Myles replied.

"I will try," Heather answered.

"I will meet you at home later. I have a lot of work to do tonight, and I am pretty sure I will be up late. I have a career-changing presentation tomorrow, and believe it or not, it is to Cheryl. I will have to tell you about it later."

"I thought the big presentation was to Vista Health. What happened with the meeting that gets us to sunset at the Eiffel Tower?" Heather asked.

"It went really well. I will have to tell you about that later, too. I am going to be late to Brickland Community Theatre if I don't go right now."

Myles was alone with his thoughts as he drove to the Brickland Community Theatre. He couldn't stop thinking about his son and his basketball game. At one point, he wondered if he should go to the meeting, excuse himself, and go to his son's game. The thought kept working its way into his mind. But he realized they were too far apart, and the travel time would make it too difficult to pull off.

As Myles was pulling into the parking lot at the Brickland Community Theatre, his phone vibrated, and he looked down to see he had received new emails. He quickly scanned through the emails and noticed one from Ted. He opened the email:

Just wanted to make sure you received my gift today. I forgot to tell you about that when we spoke on the phone. I arranged for our courier service to deliver it today. I hope you don't mind me sending that over along with the ArrowHead explanation to your office.

Ted

Myles worked hard at focusing on the Brickland Community Theatre meeting. They really were in a dilemma, and they needed everyone's help to try to solve the problem. After about ninety minutes, they had devised a very realistic plan with an ArrowHead for the donors and a StoryArc about a donor who was trying to decide whether to give to the Brickland Community Theatre or the community college. Brickland would use the ArrowHead and StoryArc at an upcoming fundraising event that could potentially solve much of their financial problems. Everyone willingly accepted their assignments and agreed to meet the following week to report on final preparations for the promotion. Solving problems was second nature for Myles, and he loved seeing a solution like this coming together.

Since Brickland Community Theatre was at the opposite end of the city, it would take Myles a while to drive home. Myles knew that Heather and Jake would arrive at about the same time he got home, and he wondered what mood Jake would be in when he saw him.

As Myles pulled up, he noticed they had already arrived. He loaded up his arms with some of the items from work and walked in the door.

"So, Jake, did you win?" Myles asked with enthusiasm, hoping it would help break any tension.

"Nope," Jake replied with a one-word answer. He didn't wait for any further conversation; he simply picked up his homework and headed with drum-like beats of his feet up the stairs to his room.

"Jake, dinner will be ready in about a half hour," Heather said.

There was no reply as Jake headed up the stairs.

"I take it he didn't take your explanation too well," Myles said, looking at Heather.

"He looked at me and said, 'What's new?' and then rolled his eyes and hasn't said much since then." Heather busied herself preparing dinner.

"So fill me in on the Vista Health lunch," Heather changed the subject, not wanting to wait to hear what happened.

Myles sat at the counter and gave his full attention to Heather. He figured since the tension was high in their home, it wouldn't help if he started into his work too quickly, so he took a deep breath and took his time telling Heather all the events of the day.

As Myles explained each detail of the lunch meeting and the request by Cheryl for his presentation, Heather was clued in to his every word. She was not only interested in what happened, but she was truly intrigued by the new methods Myles was trying. When Myles told her about the ArrowHead in a box, she stopped her meal preparation and said, "You mean he sent that to you with a complete explanation? Doesn't that seem a little weird to you that someone you haven't seen in years would send you such a gift?"

"Not at all. Ted and I spent over four years together. Almost every day we were doing something together. We obviously lost track of each other, but Ted has always been a nice guy. He just wants me to succeed. To be honest, the thing that is weird is how much of a great exec he has turned into. It's obvious I am learning from him right now," Myles replied.

"Well, if nothing else, it has given you a spark that I haven't seen in a long time. I'm grateful to him for that," Heather concluded.

Dinner was ready, and needless to say, it was pretty quiet around the table. Myles tried to get Jake to talk about the game, but Jake had an attitude and was letting the whole family know how he felt. His attitude was a weight that was dragging the family down as well. As Myles finished desert, he could feel his emotions starting to bubble over. He wanted to tell Jake how immature his actions and emotions were, but he knew it would only explode into a fight, and he selfishly didn't need a fight on that particular night.

Heather finished helping with homework, the kids went to bed, and then Myles started into his presentation. He had to figure out a way to incorporate what he had learned and communicate it to Cheryl in a way that she believed what he was saying would work, and more importantly, so she would get on the wagon and be an advocate for using the Triad Test, StoryArc, and ArrowHead.

Myles kept coming back to the ArrowHead, and he went through a number of purposes and goals for the meeting with Cheryl. The best way to explain the ArrowHead Tools was to use them with Cheryl. He needed an ArrowHead for the meeting and a story that conformed to the StoryArc, and he needed to make sure what he was presenting passed the Triad Test.

It didn't matter how many ideas he put down, bullet points he noted, or examples he wanted to cover. His mind kept coming back to the conflict with Jake. Myles really wanted to go up to Jake's room and explain why he missed another game and let him know that his actions at the dinner table weren't appropriate. But, deep down, Myles knew he couldn't be too hard on a fourteen-year-old boy, especially a fourteen-year-old boy who was disappointed in his dad for missing another basketball game.

"Why not?" Myles said out loud to himself. "Why not?" The thought crossed Myles's mind that he would make an ArrowHead for improving his relationship with his son and apply all the ArrowHead Tools he had learned. Myles remembered in the note from Ted that the ArrowHead could work for purposes in one's personal life. This is it, Myles thought, I will try the ArrowHead principle with Jake. He wondered if the struggle with Jake could be considered a "story war." The more he thought about it, the more he felt it was a war, but not one that he would win and Jake would lose. Rather, it was a war where both he and Jake would win or both he and Jake would lose; this certainly was worth his best effort.

Myles drew an ArrowHead on the paper in front of him. He looked at the note from Ted that contained the ArrowHead. He knew the top part, or point, was the main purpose, the goal, or the unique value proposition. He scribbled a few ideas on a piece of paper, and then with a pencil, he circled the last one he wrote down and neatly transcribed it at the top of the ArrowHead: "Relationship with Jake like my father had with me."

Now what would be the supporting goals to make that happen? he wondered. After jotting down some more ideas on another piece of paper, he looked at the picture of Jake and him when Myles was the assistant coach of his Little League baseball team. Myles then stared at the picture of his dad and him on his eighteenth birthday. The plan began to crystallize.

"One-on-One Time Together," Myles wrote down for the first blade of his new ArrowHead with Jake. Myles knew that part of the success with his relationship with his dad were the many one-on-one's they shared. Fishing, hiking, business trips with his dad when he was young, personal visits as Myles reached critical milestones in his own life—these were all part of the brickwork that formed the foundation of that great father-son relationship.

"Listen First" was the second blade. What Myles always loved best about his dad was that he was always there to listen. Myles was prone to lecture first and listen last. But his dad listened with the attentiveness of a hawk. He would repeat back what he had heard and ask questions when he didn't understand. When his dad did speak, it was normally in short, meaningful statements. Myles saw where he needed to improve.

"Be the Hero," was the last blade Myles wrote down. His dad was not always his hero. In fact, early on, his dad was almost a stranger to him, not always there for his son. But then something happened that seemed to change his father's heart, and he began to spend more time with young Myles. Since then, Myles always admired his dad. This helped raise Myles's expectations for himself. His dad was the role model in his professional, family, and personal life.

If Myles could have had an action figure or poster of a hero that he looked up to, it would be his father.

ArrowHead for Jake

Relationship With Jake Like My Father Had With Me

One-on-One Time Together

Listen First

Be The Hero

It was done. Instant clarity. Myles couldn't believe how focused his purpose had become and how easy it was to now structure the solution. It was liberating for Myles to know he only had to focus on three things and not be overburdened with the weight of many things. His ArrowHead with Jake comprised his highest priorities that he could focus on; it was important to Jake and him, it was certainly different from what he was doing now, and it could become credible if he lived it. It passed the Triad Test.

It was as though a burden had been lifted, and immediately, all kinds of ideas came to mind about the presentation to Cheryl. Myles had his laptop out, and he was flowing with ideas. Within an hour, he was ready for Cheryl.

CHAPTER 10
CHERYL'S BUY-IN

Myles had less than the optimum amount of sleep, as he lay in bed juggling his ArrowHead for Jake and his ArrowHead for Cheryl. He could feel the day's adrenaline starting to run through his veins. Today he had to change water to wine and convince Cheryl that the biggest prospect ever for Tangent Technologies required leaving behind all they held true as a company sales methodology. He needed to convince her that they should replace it with the ArrowHead Tools. Water to wine started to sound easy to Myles compared to what was ahead. If there was a positive, it was that Myles and Cheryl were going to meet without the sales staff, executives, or marketing department, just the two of them. Myles could contain the environment for this discussion.

Jake came down the stairs, saw Myles, and picked up his breakfast, as if to eat it on the go.

"Jake, listen, I am really sorry about last night. Nothing I can say will make up for missing another game. I would like to make it up to you. Really, I want to talk to you about something that could help me be a better father. How about you and I have this discussion at the AirOne Street Ball exhibition that is coming to town this weekend?"

Heather and Jake looked up from what they were doing. It was as much a shock to Heather as it was to Jake. Myles's innovative delivery just worked. He had their attention.

"What is the AirOne Street Ball exhibition?" Heather asked.

"Come on, Mom! Everyone knows what the AirOne Street Ball exhibition is. It is the street ball team that comes to town and plays some of the best players around. They are awesome," Jake said, with excitement in his voice.

"Are they like the Harlem Globetrotters?" Heather asked.

Jake said, "Who's that?"

Myles just smiled.

Jake looked at his dad and said, "That would be awesome! I'm in if you and Mom are good with it. I know those tickets are expensive."

Myles looked at Heather and said, "Well, honey, what do you think?"

"It sounds *awesome!*" she exclaimed, attempting to mirror the excitement in Jake's voice.

"OK, I will have Mom call today and get tickets. We can talk about some of my ideas when we go this weekend," Myles said with a smile.

Jake was out the door before anything else could be said, and Heather was still shocked and looking at Myles for an explanation.

"I know that came as a shock, but I have some ideas on how to solve the problem. Just trust me on this one. Can you call and get two tickets. The number is on the phone pad; I looked it up last night," Myles said as he started to gather his stuff to leave.

"Wish me luck—this could be the most important day of my entire career."

Heather reacted to Myles's comment by smiling and mouthing the words "good luck," then giving him a kiss that lasted a little longer than usual. Myles reluctantly headed out the door.

The day started normally for Myles as he worked through some pressing matters and tried not to focus on the Cheryl meeting. He figured he would need to brush up on the presentation he had prepared prior to the meeting, and as he looked at the clock, it was about that time. Like a seasoned professional, Myles carefully reviewed each of the presentation points he had for Cheryl. He spent part of the evening the night before preparing a perfectly crafted StoryArc for Cheryl, but more importantly, he had crafted the ultimate ArrowHead for the meeting as well.

Myles walked to Cheryl's office with the confidence of a gladiator. Successful or not, he knew this was the right battle to fight for his company.

"Good morning, Cheryl. You ready for our discussion?" Myles said with conviction as he walked into her office.

"I think the better question is are *you* ready?" she replied without a hesitation.

"Do you mind if I close the door? I want both of us to be very honest, and I think it would be best if we have this discussion without others hearing what is going on," Myles continued.

"That's fine," she replied, but she was curious about the secrecy.

Myles sat down on the chair and kept the presentation material to himself. He wanted to set the stage for his discussion with Cheryl.

"Cheryl, before we begin, can you tell me why you hired me?" Myles asked, but before she could answer, he asked her another question. "Can you remember my interview for this job? What about that interview made you think I was the right one to hire?" Myles continued.

"Well, let's see, if I recall, you were very qualified, but it seemed like the course of our interview took us to a conversation about fly-fishing. You and my husband are fly-fishing aficionados. In fact, I remember you telling me how fly-fishing was the reason you sold one of the biggest accounts at your prior company," she replied.

"Yep, we did have that conversation. The story was about the client who had wanted all their life to learn fly-fishing but never really took the time. Do you recall exactly how the story ended?" Myles asked.

For the next ten minutes, Cheryl and Myles visited about the story, fly-fishing, her husband's love of the sport, and how it closed a prior account for Myles.

Then Myles asked again, "So, Cheryl, why did you hire me? Was it because I was the most qualified, or was it because we connected in the interview? And be brutally honest with me."

"There were more qualified candidates than you, and to be completely honest, it was because we connected in the interview, and I felt like I understood what you could do. More importantly, I knew you would be willing to go the extra mile for the sale and you could provide what our company needed. I wanted our customers to feel that same connection with us, and I felt you could do that," Cheryl answered.

Myles hesitated for just a second to give Cheryl a chance to think about her comment.

"Oh, oh, I see where you are going with this. We are by far the most qualified software on paper when we make our presentation, but we don't connect with the buyer. Is that what you're getting at?"

Myles nodded in agreement. "Yeah, I don't think we're connecting with our buyers, but I think I know how we can fix that," Myles responded.

Cheryl continued, "OK, you have my attention; tell me more." Cheryl looked at Myles with an honest look of interest and willingness to hear him out.

Myles had delivered his opening. The story had worked perfectly, and now he had Cheryl willing to listen and learn.

For the next forty-five minutes, Myles carefully presented the Triad Test, the StoryArc, and the ArrowHead. He even crafted on the whiteboard in her office exactly what his ArrowHead and StoryArc were for the meeting with Cheryl so he could show her how it applied to the very meeting they were in. Myles was impressed. Cheryl had dropped all pretenses, and she was grasping the ArrowHead Tools and agreeing with what he was saying. Myles knew it was the correct time to discuss the price of the product.

"Cheryl, I want you to notice that, with this system, we never discuss the price of our software until they realize the full value of our offering, what they want and need. You and I both know people make business decisions based upon emotion and then find facts to justify their decisions. That is what we do. We have them make the software decision emotionally, and then we give them the facts to support it. One of those facts is the price. I think, right at that point, we could use the example of a heart surgeon. You know this example—the one where you have a loved one that needs a life-saving heart surgery. Would you immediately go out and try to find the cheapest heart surgeon to fix the problem? No, you want the best heart surgeon to save the life of your loved one. What is more central to our client's success than their caregiver service? It is the heart of their business, and we provide the best software available to keep that heart beating healthy and strong. This reframe will work, Cheryl, and I think you would admit it makes complete sense," Myles said.

Cheryl tapped her pencil as she thought about her reply.

"Even if I agreed with you, do you know how much of a huge leap this is going to be? We would have to get marketing, all of sales, and Darby to agree to this plan before we could make our presentation to Vista Health. That is going to take a huge buy-in," Cheryl said, without stating her opinion.

"Exactly, isn't that precisely what we want? We want everyone on the same page." Myles stood and walked over to the whiteboard again and drew an ArrowHead.

He drew the ArrowHead for the success of the company, outlining the purpose as "Win the Story War," and then he defined the blades of "CREATE Our Purpose," "ALIGN OUR Team," and "INNOVATIVE DELIVERY."

Win The Story War

Create Our PURPOSE

INNOVATIVE DELIVERY

ALIGN Our Team

"Cheryl, we can do this, and I believe what you have to ask yourself is, 'What if we don't do this?' We will continue to use the same method, and our competitors are going to continue to eat our lunch," Myles said in a cautionary tone. "I already know what the purpose of this software acquisition is with Vista Health. They want to focus on care giving, not compliance paperwork. Even better, I already have the perfect story for the StoryArc. It is made for Vista Health, and it will help win the story war. Really, don't you think we should go fly-fishing with this new method?" Myles knew it was time to be quiet. Cheryl never really answered his previous question, and now was the time to just sit back and let her answer the question.

Cheryl sat quietly at her desk looking at the whiteboard. Myles could tell that the discussion connected with her. He didn't fully appreciate that the increased sales pressure Cheryl was putting on him did not originate with her, as she was only the middleman, so Cheryl wanted a solution to this sales famine just as much as Myles did.

"Agreed," Cheryl said with abruptness.

Myles wasn't sure how to react to such an abrupt answer, and he just looked at her for a second.

"Myles, when you asked for this meeting, I wasn't sure I wanted to listen. In fact, I was impatient and wanted to get the process started for Vista Health. I was completely close-minded. I can't think of a harder sale than me for this meeting. And the truth is you sold me. It worked; well, I think it did. I believe we need to do exactly what your ArrowHead says on the board—win the Story War," Cheryl said.

Myles tried to hide his smile but couldn't. He had just witnessed water turning into wine.

Cheryl interrupted his happy thought by announcing, "Next stop—Everest."

"True, we are looking at a steep climb, but we might as well forge ahead," Myles replied.

Myles and Cheryl spent the next hour talking about how best to go about the task. They debated whether they should do the presentation to the marketing group, sales group, and Darby combined or if they should just sit down with Darby first and get his buy-in, and once that was completed, then they could meet with everyone else. Myles felt a big meeting would be more successful because he knew his sales team would love everything about this approach, and they would be vocal in support of the changes. Cheryl felt like it would run the risk of having the C-level folks getting blindsided and ganged up on and thought it was best to get Darby to buy-in and then, with his endorsement, roll it out to the rest of the company.

It was finally agreed on that they would call a meeting with just the CEO to give him the full discussion. If Darby agreed, then they would gather the heads of each of the involved departments, present the ideas, and brainstorm the perfect roadmap to win the Vista Health story war.

Cheryl picked up the phone to talk to Darby while Myles listened to only one side of the conversation. Myles just assumed that Cheryl would set the meeting for the next day to give them time to prepare and was completely shocked when Cheryl said, "Well, if now is the best time for you, why don't you wonder on down to my office because Myles and I are here, and we are going to need about a half hour of your time."

Myles looked at Cheryl with complete surprise, and Cheryl gave Myles a look to let him know they had no other option. Cheryl hung up the phone.

"Can't we do this tomorrow when we have more time to prepare?" Myles asked before Cheryl could say anything.

"He is traveling tomorrow, and he wanted to have the discussion right now. He is on his way down. I don't believe it will be that big of an issue. We are simply going to walk through everything we just discussed. Don't worry, Darby and I go way back, and I have a story I think fits the StoryArc nicely," Cheryl said.

Myles was uncomfortable knowing the amount of preparation, coordination, and work that should go into this meeting, but he felt his hands were tied. The time line of Vista Health and the schedule of the CEO meant this was a do-or-die situation. All he felt he could do was trust Cheryl.

"Myles, Cheryl, how are you?" Darby said as he walked in the room. Darby was about fifty-five years old and still in excellent shape. He had a strong personality and certainly had the confidence of a CEO. All of the interactions Myles had with Darby were business-oriented; he had never had an opportunity for a social gathering. Darby had the reputation of being unbending when it came to how the company did things, mostly because he was so sure of himself. He felt strongly about systems and usually wanted everything in the company to comply with the systems that were set up and according to the way it had been done for years. Darby believed in the heritage that made Tangent great. Myles did admire the fact that Darby was dedicated to having the very best product on the market. He was a hawk for software improvements, and he was always open to new acquisitions that made their software the leader in the industry, but he wasn't that way with business processes.

Cheryl wasted no time; she immediately put Darby at ease as they chatted a few minutes about their kids. It didn't take long for Darby to notice all the writing on the whiteboard.

"OK, Cheryl so what is this groundbreaking sales method, and what are all those arrowhead-looking things on the whiteboard?" Darby asked.

Myles could feel his knees and ankles tighten. He wanted so badly to lead the discussion. It was natural for a salesperson to always want to control any sales presentation. Myles mentally checked himself and forced himself to relax back into his chair.

Without the slightest hesitation, Cheryl launched into a story about the time a customer called her and Darby at midnight because the software they had just installed had crashed the company mainframe. She had the perfect hero, trials and difficulties, turning point, and resolution to the story. Then she said, "Now, Darby, before I explain the arrowheads, I want to remind you why we picked DataPoint to be our computer parts supplier." Cheryl then went on about how DataPoint was not the lowest-priced vendor, yet Darby selected them as their exclusive supplier.

It didn't take Darby long to remember that, during one of the meetings with DataPoint, the salesperson related how their supply chain resembled a well-oiled basketball team. She communicated the complete analogy to the offenses and defenses of basketball and how they work the same way. It was as though she knew Darby was a high school and college basketball jock and loved everything about basketball. Darby was enthralled by the story and reminisced his basketball days.

Then Cheryl asked, "So, Darby, why did you choose DataPoint?"

It was again like magic. Darby hesitated at first, but then was very honest with Cheryl about the fact that they connected and that the story made the difference. He knew DataPoint understood their problem, cared about Tangent, and had the ability to keep the company's supply chain moving smoothly.

Cheryl looked at Myles and said, "OK, Myles, he's yours; give him the whole solution."

Myles started with the ArrowHead and then worked his way through the StoryArc and the Triad Test. The entire time, Darby asked informed and interested questions. Every now and then, Cheryl would jump in and was Myles's advocate with why they should give this a try. Darby was engaged and willing.

As Myles answered a few final questions, Cheryl interrupted, "Darby, we want you on board with 'Winning the Story War' because we are in conversations with Vista Health and are preparing a presentation and proposal. They are going to be our target for this approach."

That only generated a whole new discussion on how the contact was made, what happened at the first lunch meeting , how Myles used the story, the time line they were moving on, how connected they were to the story, and the focus Vista Health was looking for. The whole meeting took much longer than Myles had anticipated.

"Cheryl, you know this isn't my style; I like something more regimented and traditional," Darby paused, "but my gut tells me this is the right thing to do. We should focus on this, and we should ramp up the presentation for Vista Health. Myles, you are the lead on this. Have they talked to our tech people yet, and do we know where we stand?" Darby asked.

"That is happening this week, and they will let us know next week if we are finalists," Myles replied.

"We are going to assume we are a finalist, and we are going to prepare for our presentation immediately." Darby was an "all-in" kind of a guy, and when he made the decision, it was obvious they were going to pursue this with a passion. There was no turning back.

"We need to make this presentation to sales, marketing, finance, and probably IT as well. Everyone needs to be on the same page and have the same ArrowHead." Myles pointed to the ArrowHead he had drawn.

"Agreed, I am cancelling my travel plans for tomorrow. We are going to work on this instead. We will prepare the meeting and information for all the department heads, and we will call a meeting with everyone the next day. Once we are all on the same page, we are going to get our research together, fine-tune the story and the presentation, and work with the Triad Test. And, Myles, if you have any more tips or tricks to this system, I want them tomorrow," Darby said in a CEO-like fashion.

Myles didn't mind if Darby viewed them as "tips or tricks" as long as he used them. He was beginning to see how natural and persuasive they were. What concerned Myles the most was Darby's presentation style of circumlocution; Darby's idea of an "elevator pitch" was designed for a mile-high skyscraper with a slow elevator.

Myles couldn't believe his ears. They cordially ended the meeting and set up a time for the next day to meet. Myles walked back to his office thinking he had either done the greatest thing ever for the company or had just sealed his fate and would be out of a job soon. He thought to himself, *Nothing like ecstasy and terror in the same moment.*

CHAPTER 11

SPIKES

A s Myles walked into his office, he was sure he would have a full day of work ahead. He needed to follow up with his staff on a few key presentations they were making that week and ensure that the ship was still moving forward despite the pending changes.

He saw a text message from Heather:

I luv what u did 4 Jake this am. Anxious to hear @ Cheryl mtg. Can't wait 2 c u 2nite! xo :).

Myles understood the not-so-cryptic message.

Myles settled into his chair and jiggled the mouse to bounce his computer screen back to life and opened his email to start triage.

"Spikes" was the subject line of the very first email. Myles had forgotten all about Ted's comment about Spikes, and just the slightest amount of panic set in as he wondered if he had left out a critical part of the concept with Spikes. He clicked on what appeared to be a fairly small email and opened it up:

Myles,

I've had one of the greatest days ever. My sales team completely aced a huge presentation. I am so proud of everyone on my team and their preparation and presentation. We went out after the meeting to celebrate, and now I am back in the hotel and remembered you have a big presentation coming up. I believe I owe you an explanation on Spikes and how to use them to "spike" your presentation and story.

Spikes are the fourth ArrowHead Tool. Think of your buyer's attention like a telephone line over a mile stretch of road. Every two hundred feet or so there is a telephone pole to hold up the line. They are evenly spaced and keep the line from touching the ground and killing people.

Spikes are like the telephone poles that hold up the telephone lines. They hold up the buyer's attention and keep it from falling to the ground and killing your deal; therefore, every presentation needs Spikes to get the listener's attention and to reconnect them with your message. Spikes are techniques you can use to make your message stick.

Every presentation you make needs a Spike now and then, something that peaks the listeners attention. I think you would agree that twelve minutes is the maximum amount of attention a listener has before their thoughts start to wonder and they begin thinking about what they'll watch on TV that night.

By "stick"—I like how the Heath brothers described it in their book, Made to Stick—I mean three things: 1) Your ideas are understood, 2) They remember it, and 3) It changes their opinion or behavior, meaning they buy your product. Spikes help your message stick. You can use a Spike anytime or anywhere and with anyone.

There are six different types of Spikes, and you can remember the various Spikes with the word IQMOVS, which stands for the following:

I—Imagine

Q—Questions

M—Metaphors

O—Objects

V—Visuals or Video

S—Stories with Conflict

I have found that each of the Spikes work equally well based upon what is in my presentation. For example, I frequently use the old-time video of Abbott and Costello doing Who's on First? to prove the point of confusion in the market. It is great for proving that customers, vendors, and clients don't always communicate well and that customer service departments can work very hard and still not accomplish the goal if they don't communicate clearly. It works great every time I use that clip.

I believe the Spikes are all self-explanatory, but I will give you more examples later when we're together. They are best demonstrated. The best Spikes are those that are imaginative, creative, unexpected, or humorous. They seem to evoke the best response. They connect your audience to your message (your ArrowHead), and they bring them back to that focus. Imagine how this compares to "death by PowerPoint" presentations! But remember to practice, practice, practice, and use the Spikes wisely; too many Spikes and you'll scare your client away. Good luck with the presentation, and let me know how it goes. We'll get back together again when we I am in town.

Thanks,

Ted

Myles breathed a sigh of relief. He could now incorporate Spikes in the next day's session. He loved the Who's on First? clip idea and thought he could use that with Vista Health. Once again, Myles was inspired by how much Ted had innovated and developed himself, not only in his career, but personally as well.

Myles checked his watch and realized he had work to finish before he needed to head home. His father had checked out of the hospital, and Myles wanted to go by his dad's house on the way home. He quickly finished work, packed up his desk so it was ready for the next day, and headed out of the office to his father's house.

Myles looked forward to visiting with his dad. He drew great strength from his relationship with his father. He knew he was loved, he knew he was important to his father, and he knew his father was interested in his life.

"Dad, you aren't running a marathon this week, are you?" Myles said as he walked in the front door and saw his dad on the couch watching some television.

"Thought I would, just need someone to push my wheelchair. You up to it?" his dad quipped.

Myles and his father visited for some time, and then Myles got around to asking him about Jake and what he should do to improve as a father. Myles knew his father was aware that he and Jake were struggling in their relationship. His dad had always remained close to the grandkids, and Myles was comfortable seeking his dad's advice.

"Dad, you know that Jake has reached his teenage years, and it has become a bit of a struggle to try to connect with him. Between my work and family, I just don't seem to balance my obligations very well," Myles said.

"How do you mean?" his dad responded. He was always good with a short response and question to draw more conversation out of his son.

"Well, I remember when I was a teenager you and mom were always there for me. Life seemed so much simpler than it is today. I feel like I am juggling so many balls and I'm not doing a good job at managing the challenges. . I just can't seem to connect with Jake like you and I connected when I was young, " Myles replied.

"Son, do you mind if I tell you a story? I promise it won't be one of those long-winded ones I occasionally get wrapped up in. Once there was a father who came home from work late, and he was tired, frustrated, and hungry. He had a seven-year-old son, and the young boy looked at his dad when he sat down and said, 'Dad, how much money do you make?' The dad, frustrated, looked at his son and said, 'That is really none of your business.' The boy tried to ask again. 'Dad, how much do you in make in a whole hour at work?' The dad was pretty frustrated by this point and said, 'Twenty dollars an hour.' Then, without even a moment's hesitation, the boy asked, 'Dad, can I have ten dollars?'

"The father was impatient, and work was long and tiring that day, and he just wasn't up to dealing with a selfish seven-year-old boy. The father, aggravated, said, 'How dare you ask for so much money when I work so hard to get what we have. I can't give you that much money. You would just waste it on something that isn't important.

Son, go to your room and stay there; you shouldn't be asking for so much money.' The boy slowly made his way to his room, and the dad didn't hear from him for some time.

"Finally, the dad decided that maybe he was too harsh on the boy and would go check on him. He went upstairs and opened the door and asked his son, who was lying on the bed, if he was asleep. The boy turned over and said no. 'Son, I might have been too hard on you earlier. I am sure you want the money for some good reason. Just this once, I am going to give you the ten dollars.' The father pulled ten dollars out of his wallet and gave it to his son. The boy almost jumped for joy and lifted up his pillow.

"The father could see there was a number of dollar bills and coins under the pillow, and he was about to get mad at the boy again for asking for so much money when he already had money. The father asked with a stern voice, 'What do you need the ten dollars for?' The boy looked at his dad, gathered up all the money, handed it to him, and said, 'Dad I have been saving up for a long time. Here is twenty dollars. Can you come home on time tomorrow and play hotwheels with me for an hour?'"

Myles looked at his father. Nothing had to be said. No analogy, no need to make the point, Myles got the full message. There was an awkward silence for just a moment, and then his father spoke again.

"Myles, the father in the story was me, and you were the seven-year-old boy. That experience was like an arrow through my heart. From that moment on, I promised myself I would straighten out my priorities. I have spent the rest of my life living according to the purposes and priorities that are truly important to me. Jake only wants the same from you."

Myles sat and reflected. He couldn't remember that experience, but he did remember how he knew he was always his father's top priority, just after his mother. Myles stood, gave his father a hug, and said, "Thank you once again for teaching me what is important. I need to get home. I will call to check in on you in a few days."

"Myles, remember," his dad continued, "your purpose will drive your passion, and your passion will give you power—power to make your family what you want."

They visited just a moment longer, and then Myles headed home. The following day was critical, and he needed to be prepared for the meeting.

Myles thought about the little gem his father gave him before he left: Purpose drives passion, and passion gives power. Could this be what makes the ArrowHead so powerful? he thought. Purpose is the backbone to story. It all started to come together for Myles.

The next day, as Myles walked into Darby's office, he felt like the mission commander of Apollo 11 stepping onto the Saturn V rocket. He was about to embark on a fantastic adventure, but the ending was cloudy and unknown. There were a number of risks along the way. Everything Myles knew were merely gold nuggets from Ted. He saw Ted as the finished product, but he had never seen this actually done. Parts of it had worked wonders with Cho of Vista Health, and as he thought about it, he also realized it had worked with Jake, Cheryl, and Darby. His confidence began to grow. Just then, Cheryl joined him, and they sat down around the small conference table in Darby's office.

"Myles, this is your baby, so tell us where we start," Darby said.

Myles launched into the need to define the ArrowHead for the meeting with all the department heads. He presented the ArrowHead that Ted used with his team and wrote it on the whiteboard: "Win the Story War" was the point, and the three blades were "CREATE our Purpose," "ALIGN our Team," and finally, "INNOVATIVE DELIVERY." Myles was careful to use the word "our" so the team would own the ArrowHead. Darby and Cheryl liked where he was going.

Myles wrote "PAID" on the board for the first letters in PURPOSE, ALIGN, and INNOVATIVE DELIVERY.

Darby was quick to say, "This is the process we will use to get paid in the future."

Cheryl laughed, and they agreed it would help make their ArrowHead more memorable. They brainstormed for over an hour on the best methods for the ArrowHead to be accomplished. Once they had that down, they went to work on the stories they would use to win the story war with their team. They worked at the StoryArc, they made sure what they were presenting met the Triad Test, and then Myles spent fifteen minutes explaining that every presentation needed Spikes and made some suggestions about what they might use for them. The night before, Myles had downloaded the Who's On First? video clip to his laptop. He played it for both Cheryl and Darby, and they absolutely loved the idea. It was the perfect example of how the company was working between IT, marketing, sales, and finance. It proved the point exactly as to why they needed to come together and communicate with a common goal and purpose. Through all of their efforts, they had a wonderful flow to the presentation for their team.

Darby stood from the table and walked over to his desk. "Debbie, would you come in here please," he said into the intercom.

Debbie walked into the office and waited for instructions.

"Would you have the heads of development, IT, finance, and marketing meet in the conference room tomorrow at ten a.m.? And tell them it will be an hour-long meeting. If they ask what it is about, tell them I have some discussion points I want to cover."

Debbie stepped out of the office, and Myles, assuming the meeting was over, began to gather up his notes and papers.

"Myles, I know this may not sit well with you, but I need to be the one who gives this presentation tomorrow," Darby said, with just the slightest hint of a question in his statement.

Myles didn't know how to respond. He stood there for just a second. He thought, How do you tell your CEO that he is the wrong guy to give the presentation?

Darby could tell Myles was uncomfortable with the suggestion, so he continued, "If you give this presentation, it will look like sales has pushed this idea, and we will get some resistance from the other departments. It will also look like you are pitching me with the idea, and they will wonder if I am fully on board with the idea. If I pitch this, there is no question I am a proponent of the idea, and everyone can then discuss the issues without petty turf wars."

It made sense to Myles, but he still wondered how Darby would do with the presentation.

"I agree," Myles replied. "I just want to make sure you are OK with giving this presentation. I mean, this requires preparation, and do you have time for this?" Myles thought that was the best way he could pose the question.

"I am not ready right now, but I will be ready tomorrow at ten a.m. I have the rest of the day to get ready, and trust me, I will be ready," Darby said as he stepped behind his desk.

With that, the meeting ended, and everyone headed back to their own offices.

CHAPTER 12

COMPANY ALIGNMENT

For the most part, everyone gets along at Tangent, and they are professional and cordial. As with any company, there are underlying competitions, feelings, quiet whispers, machinations, and turf wars. In the early days, Tangent Technologies had avoided much of those problems. It was only in the last few years, as the competition stiffened and success wasn't coming as easily, that all of those problems began to surface.

It was 9:58 a.m., and Myles walked into the conference room. It was already set up, and most everyone was present. Cheryl was already seated, and Darby had just entered the room. Myles quickly turned his head and stared at Darby.

The CEO entered the room with a huge set of earmuff-like headphones on his head. They had been spray-painted bright orange; in fact, they were brighter than highway worker orange. Myles didn't know what to think.

Everyone was in the room and staring at Darby. There was an uncomfortable silence. No one knew if this was a joke, an object lesson, or worse. Myles wondered if Darby had lost his mind the night before in preparing for the meeting. Slowly, everyone sat down as if Darby was going to call the meeting to order.

Darby walked to each of the employees and put his hand out to shake their hands. He greeted them as though nothing was wrong. He walked to the head of the table, looked at Cheryl, and said, "Cheryl, do we have everything set up and ready for the meeting?"

"We do. Are you ready for the screen to come down?" Cheryl asked.

"I am sorry, Cheryl, I can't hear you. Would you mind repeating what you just said?" Darby answered.

"Darby, what are those silly headphones on for?" Cheryl finally asked what they all wanted to know.

"What headphones?" Darby didn't buy into the obvious, and his answer made everyone in the room even more uncomfortable. To make matters even worse, he didn't jump at the chance to clear things up. He started to take things from his briefcase and booted up his laptop computer while everyone sat in silence as he prepared for the meeting. Even Myles thought this was weird. He didn't think this was a great start to the meeting they had prepared, and then Darby broke the silence.

"Folks," Darby started as he slowly removed the earmuffs, "I want you to know that, for the last two years, I have symbolically worn these earmuffs every day at work, and none of you have taken the time to ask me why I couldn't hear well. I am a little disturbed by that. And the real truth is that each of you, and your departments, has also worn earmuffs. Simply put, we are not listening to our clients, we are not hearing what our competition is doing, and we are blocking out change and pushing ahead with what we have always done and how we have always gone about business. Today, in this meeting, I want you all to take off your earmuffs and listen with an open mind and a spirit of change for what is best for our clients, and ultimately, for our company."

Myles, impressed, sat back in his chair. Darby had just started the meeting with an Object Spike, and it worked. It not only worked, it worked beautifully. Myles looked around the table as Darby continued to speak, and everyone was smiling and attentive, and their defenses were down. They were willing to work. They were connected to their CEO.

After a brief introduction on what the meeting was to accomplish, Darby started the *Who's on First?* video, which was a huge hit. Everyone in the room was laughing, smiling, and completely connected to his message. Immediately following the video, Darby drove home the principle of alignment. Then, like a skilled master craftsmen,

Darby used every story, covered every purpose, motivated the team, and before it was over, he had their complete buy-in. Myles was shocked that Darby even drew an ArrowHead on the board and defined the purposes and timeline going forward. The team agreed to collaborate to find company-wide ArrowHeads, stories that would work for the upcoming Vista Health presentation and proposal.

Myles sat in awe; Darby had done a better job than he would have done. It was as if the ArrowHead of winning the Story War, supported by PURPOSE, ALIGNMENT, and INNOVATIVE DELIVERY had PAID immediate dividends. At the conclusion of the meeting, Darby asked Myles to give a quick update on the Vista Health opportunity so that they could set a time to start working on the presentation, even though they were not yet aware if they would be a finalist. Myles spent five minutes updating the team; they agreed to meet the following week to prepare, and the meeting adjourned.

"So, Myles, how did you think the meeting went?" Darby asked smugly as he approached Myles after the meeting.

"Amazing, just amazing. I must admit, I was impressed with your presentation," Myles replied.

"Great, get back to your office, and do what you have to do to ensure we are one of the finalists," Darby said, with some authority and a smile.

Thomas was already waiting for Myles when he walked into his office.

"So how did it go?" Thomas asked.

"Better than anyone ever expected. We are on for the ArrowHead Tools in selling Vista Health," Myles replied.

"That is great news. Not to rain on your parade, but I got a call from Cho at Vista, and he said their technical department had some real concerns. Because of the size and complexity of our software, they didn't think they could get it integrated with their software fast enough for the fast implementation time line they are on. Any ideas on what to do?" Thomas asked, with obvious fear in his voice.

"Yes, you get our two best systems guys on the phone, schedule to go over to Vista Health, and let them sit in a room for as long as it takes to answer all of their technical questions. I want you there, too. You do it right now, and you tell them we will spend as long as it takes to get the answers their IT guys need. This is a great opportunity for us to show how committed we are to solving problems—and solving them quickly. When you are done with that call, come back and tell me how it went and if the meeting is set to go," Myles directed.

Thomas left the office without saying another word.

Myles thought nothing would be worse than not even making it to the finalist stage. It simply couldn't happen.

"Myles, your son is on line three," Myles's admin broke into his concentration.

It was rare that his son called, and Myles thought maybe their talk the other night and his commitment to do better might have broken the ice.

"What's up, Son?" Myles asked.

"So Mom got the tickets for the AirOne Street Ball exhibition, and the only time we could do it is tomorrow night. That OK?" Jake asked.

"No problem, I will wrap things up tomorrow plenty early to make it on time," Myles replied.

"Great, also, did you remember we are in the semifinal game tonight for our regional league?" Jake asked, not wanting to come right out and ask if his dad was going to be there.

"Yep, I do. This one will be close, but I promised, and I will do my best to be there," Myles replied, and then they quickly finished the conversation. Myles knew this was a big game for his son. If they won, they would be in the regional championship game the following week, and that would be huge.

Myles started to concentrate on his work and wondered if he should call Thomas back to see what happened with the Vista Health technical meeting. Instead, he decided to give himself some time to arrange the IT solution.

"Done," Thomas stated, barging into Myles's office.

"What do you mean, done? Done good or done bad?" Myles asked.

"Done good. I am leaving right now, and I am taking Sunjay and Mia, and we are meeting with their IT folks right now. I told them we are willing to order-in dinner, stay as long as needed, and work through the issues until they are comfortable our software will integrate reliably and on schedule. Think of me as I sit there and try to help our system guys talking IT lingo all night long," Thomas said in a sarcastic tone as he turned to walk out the door.

"Myles, Cheryl would like you in her office as soon as possible," Myles's admin said over the intercom.

Myles's first thought was of the volume of work and sales calls he needed to make before the day was over. He didn't have a lot of time to sit and visit. He left his desk thinking, *This better be a productive meeting.*

"Myles, I just heard from the systems guys that we have a problem at Vista. I need you to get on the phone right now with your contact there and see if we can get a meeting set up with our systems guys and get this solved. I don't care what is on your plate; this is now job one," Cheryl said with an unjust amount of panic in her voice.

"Done. Actually, Thomas solved it. Thomas arranged for Sunjay and Mia to go with him. They are headed over to Vista Health as we speak, and both teams are working into dinner tonight to figure out the solutions. What really surprises me is the speed at which Vista Health wants to integrate this software system," Myles said with a smile.

"Great, one other thing—do you know what tonight is? It is the annual conference dinner for the National Association of Software Sales Professionals. Our company purchased a table for five thousand dollars. We have eight seats, and Darby just told me he would like you to come sit with us for the conference dinner. This is a big deal. It will be Darby and his wife, two other board members and their spouses, and then you and I have been invited. Anyone who is anyone in the industry will be at this dinner. It is a nice affair. We need to be there at six thirty. There should be enough time after work to run home, put on formal attire, and then meet at the Grand Ballroom for the dinner and meeting," Cheryl spoke matter-of-factly.

Myles knew this was huge. For him to be invited by Darby was a giant compliment and a feather in his cap. Myles could tell that even Cheryl was surprised to be invited. It didn't take long for Myles to immediately recognize the conflict with Jake's game. Myles hesitated just slightly before he answered, "Sure, I can do that. I will need to leave work a little early. I need to arrange for some video equipment before I can get home and change and be back to the dinner," Myles said, knowing that this was only a half-baked solution to Jake's game. Myles had promised that if he couldn't attend, he would at least have it videotaped, and then he could sit with Jake and watch the game together. That would just have to do for tonight.

Myles called his wife once he was back in his office and explained the situation and told her he would be home early. He intended to actually get changed, have the family drive two cars to Jake's game, set up the video recorder for Heather, and get it ready to go, and then he would leave to the dinner, and they could come home after the game and watch the tape with Jake. At least this way Jake would see him making the effort to get the game on tape.

Jake listened to the plan, and Myles could tell he was disappointed, yet at the same time, Jake could also tell his dad was making an effort, which was an improvement. Myles could also see the disappointment in Jake's eyes, and it was painful for a father to see. But Jake was really good at not saying anything and just agreeing to the plan.

The plan worked pretty well, and at 6:05, Myles left the gym in his formal attire and headed to the hotel for the dinner. Myles walked in right at 6:30, and the company table already had everyone seated, awaiting the events of the evening. Myles took the time to look around. He estimated there were over five hundred people being served, and it was kind of a who's who of the software industry. It wasn't exactly his style, but the evening turned out well with good music, an entertaining speaker, and absolutely great food.

As the evening concluded, Myles knew it was important company politics that he had accepted the invitation, and at the same time, he kept thinking about his dad's story and the twenty dollars an hour.

"Dad, guess what? We won!" Jake said as Myles walked through the door.

"That is great! Did you get the entire game taped?" Myles asked.

"Believe it or not, Mom figured it out, and we have the whole thing on tape. It is an awesome game; it had to be better than your stuffy dinner," Jake said, with the right amount of excitement and a twinge of sadness that, again, his dad missed another game.

"Eat your dinner, and then you and I will watch the game and see if there is anything in the tape that can help you get ready for the big championship game next Thursday," Myles said as he walked over to the kitchen table.

CHAPTER 13

THE FINALISTS

There was energy at work. The new week brought with it new perspective. News had spread like wildfire. The ArrowHead and the StoryArc were all people could talk about. It was an amazing thing, as not a single thing had changed in the company financial or business status. The outside world knew nothing of the pending changes inside Tangent Technologies. The new week did not bring with it a large new account, more profits, better benefits, or improved working conditions. What it did bring was hope and purpose. It was like the whole company was buzzing about Darby's meeting last week. Even the tech guys who never seemed to care about marketing, sales, or finance were interested in what was happening. Darby's presentation had turned the company on end. Those who were in the meeting were asked questions over and over again, and those who weren't in the meeting wanted to know every detail. Hope is a drug that not only sustains life, but also hallucinates happiness. Myles was amazed at how the meeting and the change in direction had affected the entire company. And the change came voluntarily; it did not have to be forced.

Mondays at Tangent Technologies generally start pretty slow. As everyone gathers from the weekend, it takes them a while to get back into the swing of things, generate momentum, and start the work process all over again. It was like an old steam engine that took a few slow chugs before it finally got going. This Monday, however, was much different. Myles was generally the first member of the sales staff in the office. As Myles walked down the hall, he noticed a few lights were already on, and work was already happening.

The surprise of all surprises for Myles was that Thomas was already in his office. As Myles walked by, he heard Thomas say, "Myles, don't walk past my door; I have news."

Myles did an about face and turned around to stand in the doorway of Thomas's office.

"It is too early to have news," Myles said.

"Nope, I got a call last night, and Cho wanted to go grab a bite with me. Actually, he wanted to play racquetball, but we couldn't get a court reserved on such late notice, so we just decided to go to dinner," Thomas said in his usual loquacious way.

Myles stepped out of the doorway and into the office and sat in the chair across from Thomas.

"Keep going," Myles said impatiently

"Do you want the short version or the long version?" Thomas asked.

"I want the good-news version!" Myles said with even more impatience.

"Well, I learned what the rush was for this decision to adopt new software for Vista Health. Cho was more than forthcoming during our dinner. It seems, a few months ago, they were hit with a pretty sizable lawsuit. Apparently, a client-patient of theirs died in their home, and the cause of death may be linked back to the quality of care provided by Vista. Cho felt like they wouldn't have a problem with the lawsuit. But what worried them is that in auditing the care provided by the company, they found all kinds of errors in the paperwork, tracking, and coding of the services. It didn't stop there; this same employee had caused a number of Medicare billing problems. It became a snowball once they started looking at the detail of this incident. They found so many flaws in the system that they immediately brought in Dayal, their chief of client services, and put him on the hot seat. According to Cho, Dayal pulled out memo after memo requesting the company improve systems and update technology to avoid exactly what was happening. It appears Dayal is now the hero since he had been pushing the change for some time. Anyway, long story short, this appears to be the reason the company is all-hands-on-deck and wants to get software in place before they have another damaging issue." Thomas leaned back in his seat like he was the holder of confidential information and wanted Myles to beg for more.

"Vista Health is huge. If they found one caregiver with so many problems, there have to be many, many more with paperwork errors, billing code errors, and quality-of-care issues. That could be devastating to Vista," Myles said, hoping Thomas would tell him more.

Thomas continued, "They have rallied all their internal resources, and they are burning the midnight oil looking at every option and solution to the problem."

"That is great news! I am happy to hear they want to move quickly," Myles replied.

"That is why our effort to get over to their company with our systems guys on Friday night and spend all the time necessary to answer their questions was so valuable. They loved our responsiveness, and it appears they solved most of the problems. As I understand it from Sunjay and Mia, our solution will take longer than some of the other solutions to implement, but they are satisfied they can get it integrated with all of their existing software and systems in time," Thomas said with a smile.

"Great news! That is great news on a Monday morning!" Myles stood to leave his office.

"I'm not done... Cho told me we are one of three finalists, and we need to be ready for a presentation later this week. He will call with a day and time. They want us to have a full pitch to give to their executive team." Thomas had held that great news until he knew it would come as a surprise to Myles.

"Wow, that is fantastic news! No wonder you are in early today." Myles reached across the desk to shake Thomas's hand and congratulate him on the great news.

"Well, don't just sit there! This is your account, so let's go tell Cheryl and Darby. They deserve to hear the news from you," Myles said as he started to motion for Thomas to follow him over to the C-suite.

Thomas was obviously proudly uncomfortable as they made their way to Darby's office. Myles didn't feel it was proper to barge into Darby's office without Cheryl in tow, so they stopped by her office first and quickly asked her to come along, as they had an announcement they wanted to share with Darby.

Darby had just walked into the office, and his admin didn't hesitate to send them in, especially since Cheryl was with them.

"Darby, Thomas has some news he wants to share," Cheryl said.

"Sir, we are finalists. On Friday night, Cho confirmed we are one of the finalists, and they will let us know when we need to have our presentation and proposal ready. He said it would probably be later this week," Thomas said with pride.

"Oh, the dulcet tones of success!" Darby always had a way with words; he was elated, but also oddly inquisitive. He asked Thomas to share everything about the dinner meeting, and it was over a half hour before they got out of his office. Before they left, Darby had coordinated the preparation meeting for the team. He pointed to Myles and said, "Myles, you are going to lead this presentation, so get your A-game skills ready to go." And then Darby looked at Cheryl and said, "Cheryl, we have to be prepared with a price. There is no way to avoid the question when it comes up in the presentation. I would like to meet with you and the IT team this afternoon. They should have a good idea of what implementation is required, and we need to be prepared with a price."

The word "price" stopped Myles in his tracks. He knew they would be higher than everyone else. *We can handle price. We need to be prepared with a*

StoryArc, an ArrowHead, and a good response on how to handle the price question when it comes up, he thought. Gradually, he began to settle back into an reserved confidence, despite ending the conversation on the word "price."

With price in the back of Myles's head, he wanted nothing more than to do this presentation. He was confident that, with the new approach and his ArrowHead, he could hit a home run with this presentation. He wanted to be the one to handle the whole price question when it came up. It was agreed by everyone that Tuesday was preparation day. Darby asked Thomas to push Cho just a little to see if he could find out when they would be presenting and who the other finalists were in the process.

There was plenty of work to do. It was still Monday morning, and the rest of the staff had sales calls to make, questions to be answered, and the company still needed to move forward. Even the smallest prospect deserved the best the company had to offer. Myles and Thomas went back to their office and back to work. Myles called his admin in to work on his calendar for the week. She sat down and started to rattle off his scheduled appointments, calls, and meetings.

"I need to make sure I have tomorrow open for the prep meeting on the Vista Health deal. I also need to make sure nothing spills over into Thursday night. It is my son's championship basketball game, and I have promised myself, on my own life, I will make that game," Myles said. He continued, "I believe we will have a Thursday or Friday presentation at Vista Health, so why don't we keep both of those open for now."

Myles gave his admin a number of tasks to follow up on, and as she left the office, he picked up the phone to call Heather. Heather hadn't shown any disappointment about the trip to Paris and did all she could to buoy Myles's confidence. In fact, she had never brought it up again, and Myles felt like it would be the right thing to do to keep her posted on the progress. They both knew this account would mean not only Paris, but also any other trip they wanted to take.

The day went as planned, and before long, Myles was headed home for the evening. It was all he could do not to pre-brainstorm ideas for the Tuesday prep meeting. He wanted this to be a collaborative process and an alignment meeting, so he didn't want to bias the presentation preparation with his preconceived thoughts. Even then, he couldn't stop all the synapses from firing.

The next morning, everyone involved in the Vista Health opportunity gathered in the conference room. Darby announced that Myles would give the presentation and the meeting was to structure the presentation around an ArrowHead that Myles would lead the team to create.

Myles started with a few thoughts on the whiteboard, then asked the team to pitch in about what they thought their unique value would be to Vista. He could feel the floodgates beginning to open. The fire hose was open and years of pent-up ideas started to flow. Much to Myles surprise, even the marketing department had great ideas. Sunjay and Mia had learned in their technical dinner with Vista that the other two finalists were from out of town and out of state; only Tangent was the local finalist. The meeting went extremely well. Myles had drawn a blank ArrowHead on a flipchart and tore it off and put it on the front wall.

Myles asked the group, "What exactly does Vista Health need from our software?"

After a few comments, Cheryl said it best: "Free to focus on care giving, not paperwork."

Myles wrote it at the top of the ArrowHead after everyone nodded in agreement. He remembered sharing those words with Cheryl in recapping their visit with Cho; these were the words that Vista's chief of client services used when he told Cho what they needed. Using their own words seemed like a good idea.

It wasn't long until they had the three blades to their ArrowHead:

1. Easy and Accurate Data Entry
2. Watertight Compliancy
3. Fast Local Support

When Myles saw everyone nodding their heads in agreement, he knew this was a good ArrowHead for the Vista presentation. Myles validated it with the team by putting the words "What if you…" in front of each element of the ArrowHead. He told the team, "now imagine you are the Vista buying committee and you heard the following," and he read the ArrowHead with "what if you" in front of each blade. Myles liked the looks on their faces.

ArrowHead for Vista Health

Free To Focus
On Caregiving, Not Paperwork

**Easy &
Accurate Data
Entry**

**Watertight
Compliancy**

**Fast Local
Support**

The focus then shifted to the Spikes, and the team's ideas were so creative it shocked Myles. One of the IT guys came up with a Spike for the third blade, "Fast Local Support," which was to close the presentation by having each Tangent team member put his or her car keys in the center of the conference room table; the presenter would then say, "This is how we all got here today. We each drove our own cars. We challenge you to ask the other finalists to show their keys, and you will likely see rental car keys and taxi receipts. What this means to you is that when there is an issue, we will be here in a matter of minutes, rather than hours and days." Myles loved the passion he was seeing in his team.

The stories they settled on were excellent and had wonderful StoryArcs. They were all speaking the same language. It seemed to be working like a well-oiled machine. They were just starting to cover how to handle potential objections or issues that would be raised in the presentation when Thomas poked his head in the conference room.

"Sorry to interrupt, I just heard back from Cho. We are on for Thursday night at six p.m. for our presentation, and our two competitors are Advanced Health Solutions and XM3 Software," Thomas said with a huge smile.

"That seems a little late for a presentation. Doesn't that seem a little odd?" Darby shot back.

"We are last, and it was the only time they could make their schedules work. Are we OK with that?" Thomas asked.

"We'll make it work. You tell them we will be ready. Please make sure they have a whiteboard available and the tech plug-ins we need for our presentation," Darby said.

"Already done," Thomas replied as he left the room.

Myles couldn't believe what he just heard—Thursday at 6:00 p.m. *It just couldn't be*, he thought to himself. Myles wondered what the odds were of an afterhours presentation on Thursday night, the very night of Jake's championship basketball game. Myles tried to gather himself and contain his thoughts so he could conclude the meeting. His mind was racing trying to figure out how he was going to tell Jake.

"Myles, you with us?" Cheryl said, shocking Myles back into the conversation.

"Just thinking about a few too many issues," he replied.

The meeting began to break up, and everyone was all a clamor about the opportunity and the plan. Myles gathered his items and started to head back to his office. All he could think about was the conflict with the date and time. He wondered if he had done the right thing by not saying anything right when Thomas announced the time. Myles was completely absorbed in his thoughts as he passed a few employees without even acknowledging their greeting.

Myles sat in his office chair and contemplated what he should do. Jake had heard every excuse in the book. Myles remembered his dad's story, and he thought about his ArrowHead commitment he had made to himself and his son. He even started to scratch numbers on a pad on his desk to estimate what his portion of the commission would be on this Vista deal. The numbers were almost too much to consider.

Myles glanced at the ArrowHead and thought back to the AirOne Street Ball event. Jake was the most talkative he had been with Myles in months. Not only was it great for the two of them to watch the event, it was even better for Myles to see how much of a difference it meant to Jake that his dad had dedicated time just for him. Myles opened the box with the ArrowHead and gently fingered the blades of the arrow. On the back of Ted's note was a quote from Antoine de Saint-Exupéry; Myles recognized the name as the author of *The Little Prince*. The quote seemed an apt description of the ArrowHead: "You know you've achieved perfection in design, not when you have nothing more to add, but when you have nothing more to take away."

Myles knew the decision would not be easy, but he knew what he had to do.

CHAPTER 14

HOW DID YOU CHANGE THE WORLD?

Myles decided it would be best not to call Heather and explain the situation. He knew that this would be a long conversation and one he should have in person with her. He knew she also had a vested interest in this decision. There was a strong possibility that if Myles didn't do the presentation, they wouldn't win the account, which meant no bonus, no Pinnacle club, and no sunset on the Eiffel Tower with Heather. Those were all thoughts that Myles didn't feel he could discuss over the phone.

Myles pulled his car very slowly into the garage. He checked his watch and saw it was about 6:30. Dinner would be waiting, and the kids were probably impatient by now, waiting for him and dinner. He took note of the sign that Heather had put on the door from the garage into the house that said, "The most important work I can do in my life happens on the other side of this door." Myles almost never noticed that sign she had put up years ago, but that night, every word glared at him. Home and family were Heather's passion, and Myles was always working to keep them in balance with his work. Myles took a deep breath, then gathered his briefcase and slowly walked into the house. He didn't want to let the kids know that he was burdened by work. Jake would obviously be excited about the championship game, and he wanted the dinner to go normally.

After dinner, homework was completed, and the kids were finally in bed.

"Heather, do you have a minute? I want to run a situation by you," Myles asked, with some hesitation.

"Sure, what is it?" she replied.

"Lets go sit on the porch; it's nice out tonight and we can chat outside," Myles said.

Myles and Heather stepped outside the house. The front porch was small, but it was big enough for two chairs to sit at an angle to each other. They both sat down, and Heather could sense that something was pretty serious for Myles.

She started to worry and quickly asked, "What is it? You look worried."

"The day went perfectly today. You wouldn't believe what we accomplished. It was like everyone was singing from the same songbook. We prepared the biggest presentation in company history in about two hours, and everyone from each of the departments was on the same page. It was almost magical. In fact, if you can believe this, Blake from marketing—you remember, "Bleak Blake"—even came up to me during a break and said he was very impressed with the whole new concept.

"So we are about ready to wrap up everything. We had just finished the discussion on how to handle the question of pricing—by the way, you won't believe how we are going to handle the pricing issue. The story we have prepared for the pricing objection is really brilliant. I don't even think we will need it because they will recognize the value, and pricing will be secondary. Anyway, just as we are getting ready to wrap things up, Thomas sticks his head in the door and says the presentation has been scheduled with Vista Health for Thursday at six p.m." Myles leaned back in his chair so Heather could take in the magnitude of the conflict.

Heather hesitated just briefly and then realized that Jake's championship game was that night.

"You have got to be kidding! Are you serious?" she replied.

"I didn't say anything to anyone at work. I wanted to think about it for a while, and then I knew I needed to come home and talk about this before any decision was made," Myles replied.

Heather was still a little stunned, and Myles could tell she was trying to process the problem and decide what was the best thing to do.

"So is anyone else in the company assuming they are giving this presentation, or is it you?" she asked.

"It's me. That is one of the problems. I am the one who has lobbied hard for this new concept, got everyone on the same page, and really, there isn't anyone else in the company who can do this presentation. Obviously, I can't turn this over to Thomas. I don't think Cheryl would do a good job. I mean, really, it is me or a probable disaster," Myles replied. Myles shifted in his seat because he was a little uncomfortable with claiming he was the only one.

"So what happens if you tell them you won't be available at that time and someone else has to do it?" Heather asked.

"I think Cheryl goes crazy, Darby puts all the pressure in the world on me, and I think this is my job-on-the-line type of decision. It is the biggest account in the history of our company. It isn't going to go over well," Myles replied.

"OK, so what are the chances that you could get the presentation time moved?" Heather asked as if she were grasping for straws.

"Not a chance. They have all three presentations lined up, and we are last one, which is exactly the position we want to be in. It's not even a consideration to move the time," Myles replied.

Heather twirled her hair in her fingers. Myles knew that was a sign of frustration, and he could see that she understood the full magnitude of the problem.

"I guess we could videotape his championship game and then bring it home and watch it like the last one. Jake seemed OK with that, and after you two were done watching the game, I think he kind of liked the chance to talk through what he did well and could have done better," Heather said.

"Or I could videotape my presentation, and Cheryl could explain the situation and then play the tape for the Vista Health presentation," Myles said sarcastically. Gathering his sobriety, Myles returned by saying, "Yea, I thought about that, but we just had that huge talk with Jake about getting my priorities straight, spending one-on-one time together, listening first, and being the hero. Seems like I am copping out if I just tape the game," Myles said.

"We are talking about the biggest commission we have ever made, job security, and a trip to Paris. Myles, this is big!" Heather said as if to reiterate the size of the problem.

"Your singing to the choir here, honey. You don't need to tell me what this means," Myles replied, with a measured amount of the obvious coming out in his voice.

Both transfixed with catatonic stares, they sat in silence for a moment while thinking through what to do. Heather was really torn between the two options. She had spent the last two or three years trying to get Myles to value his role as a father more and sacrifice his time for the children. She had performed a very fine balancing act between supporting him and his work and trying to raise a family with the same closeness, values, and love that she grew up with. This wasn't an easy decision for Heather, and now she was faced with what seemed to be a no-win situation.

"Myles, I know this isn't much help, and I don't want to make this any harder for you than it already is, but to be honest, I don't know what to tell you. I don't know what you should do," Heather said with complete honesty.

"I told myself that my personal goal and purpose that I needed to work on was to have a relationship with Jake as good as my father had with me. I can't honestly say I am going to accomplish that goal if every time there is a big conflict, I fall back on doing what is needed at work and not what is needed at home. I know this sounds weird, but no success at work can offset my family's happiness. I really believe that, and I need to find that balance in my life. I need to put first things first, and now is the time. It is weird. I am talking myself into telling them tomorrow I can't do this presentation, and the more I talk, the more it feels right, and the more committed I am to that decision. I mean, I am making it as we talk. I am going to go into work tomorrow and tell Cheryl and Darby of my decision, and I am going to be at Jake's game on Thursday night," Myles said. He couldn't believe how committed he was to that decision after he said it.

Heather looked at him in surprise. Even she didn't know what to say and was very torn, but as she listened to Myles, she could hear the conviction in his voice. "Wow, you really mean it. I think you have your decision. You know I will support your decision. I hope you are able to get some sleep tonight. You can't be a mess tomorrow when you show up to make this announcement," Heather said.

They visited for a few more minutes about the activities of the week and then decided to go inside because it was getting chilly on the porch.

The alarm didn't even need to go off. Myles had been staring at it for an hour. He reached over and turned it off just as it started to ring. Myles reluctantly got ready for the day and started out the door.

Heather stopped him as he was leaving and said, "Call me the second it is over."

"The second what is over?" Jake asked. He had overheard her comment and wondered what they were talking about.

"Nothing, I just have a big meeting today, and Mom wants to know how it goes," Myles jumped in. He didn't want Jake to know anything about the conflict. Myles knew it wouldn't be fair to worry Jake about any sacrifice that was happening prior to the big game. Jake needed to just be happy they were coming to the game and not worried his dad was stressed out over a decision to attend because of work.

It was just like the start of any other workday. Myles started with his email messages, worked his way to voicemail, and then took the time to calendar his appointments. As 10:00 rolled around, he knew it would be better to have this conversation early so they could develop a backup plan. It was a courtesy he needed to afford management. He stood and started toward Cheryl's office. Just as he was getting ready to leave his office, he heard the ding of an email arriving. That was nothing new since Myles received about a hundred emails a day. Normally, Myles wouldn't have even hesitated, but for some reason, he paused and walked back to the computer. The email prompt on the screen said, "How did you change the world?" and he noticed it was from Ted. Myles sat down, moved the mouse, clicked on the email, and started to read:

Myles,

I hope you don't mind if I share one other thing with you that has helped me as I worked my way through the world of business. A few years back, I was visiting my family. I hadn't seen them in some time. It was summertime, and my sister was also in town to visit our parents. It was great to be around family again, especially my sister. She has three girls, and I must say, my nieces are very cute. Well, her youngest was about eleven years old at the time. She was born with a physical disability and has always had trouble walking. She just can't keep up with the other kids. It has caused her to be very patient and a little more reflective. It pulls my heartstrings every time I see her.

Anyway, we were sitting on our porch, and the other two were playing tag in the yard. She climbed up on my lap and said, "Uncle Ted, have you ever done something really important?" I didn't know how to answer her question, and to be honest, I didn't think I had ever done anything really important in life. I looked at her with some concern, and then she shot me a question that hit me like a lightning bolt: "How did you change the world?" I didn't know what to say. I wasn't sure anything I had done in life really made a difference to the world, or more importantly, to anyone in the world. I just sat there dumbfounded, and she eventually climbed off my lap and went to try to play tag with her sisters.

That question has really stuck with me, and I often ask myself if what I am doing today will make a difference in the world or a difference in anyone else's world. It has given me pause as I consider how I spend my time and what I spend my time on. So, I ask you the same question.

How did you change the world?

Best of luck in all you do. I truly wish you the best.
Ted

Myles sat back in his chair. Never before had he felt so good about his decision to not do the presentation. He knew from his conversation with Heather the night before that it was the right thing to do, but after reading Ted's email, he was supremely confident that it would make a difference in Jake's life. Going to his championship basketball game would be a meaningful contribution to their lifelong relationship. There would be many other "Vista Healths" and other "Tangent Technologies" in the years to come, but this moment for his fourteen-year-old's championship game would only come once.

Myles chose not to answer Ted's email, and he stood with confidence and headed toward Cheryl's office.

"Do you have a minute?" Myles said as he poked his head around the corner of Cheryl's office.

"Sure, come on in," she replied.

"How about we both drop in on Darby? I have something I want to discuss with of the two of you," Myles motioned for Cheryl to join him as they walked down the hall to the corner office.

Darby's admin was more than willing to show them in, and they sat on the couches in the corner sitting area.

"So I don't want to send shock waves through our presentation, but I have a family conflict with the presentation time on Thursday at six p.m., and I can't make it. I need to pass on the opportunity to present to Vista Health," Myles said with conviction.

Immediately, Cheryl stood up and replied, "It isn't an opportunity to present; it is a must, a requirement, not an option! What could possibly be a family conflict that you can't make it? It simply has to be moved so you can do the presentation."

"My fourteen-year-old son Jake is playing in the championship basketball game for the regional finals. Work has kept me from every game he has had this season, and I have promised him I would attend this game, and it is a promise I intend to fulfill," Myles said in a calm voice.

"This just isn't going to work. You have to make arrangements to make the presentation. Surely your son will understand. I would be happy to explain to him why you can't make it. We will even send the company video tech people over to tape the game for you. I don't think you understand. There isn't an option. You need to make arrangements to make this presentation." Cheryl's shrill voice was starting to increase in intensity.

Myles had anticipated such a response from Cheryl, so he decided to explain why he had to go. In a tone that was soft and deliberate, Myles responded, "A few weeks back, I spent the better part of an evening working on my own personal ArrowHead. I came to the conclusion that the thing that needed the most help, improvement, and work in my life was my relationship with my son. During the course of that night, I determined my personal ArrowHead would be to have the same relationship with my son that my father had with me. To be honest, my relationship with my father is something I treasure above all else. I don't have that with my son. Things have been a little rough lately, and I have committed to my ArrowHead. I simply feel it is the right thing to go to the game and let someone else give the presentation."

"I understand your commitment, and I admire what you are doing, but Myles, we don't have 'someone else' to give this presentation. You can fulfill the commitment to your ArrowHead starting Friday morning. This really isn't an option. You need to do this presentation," Cheryl said as she looked at Darby for support.

During this entire conversation, Darby sat quietly, listening intently to everything that was being said. Myles was surprised that Darby hadn't jumped in to join Cheryl in the tongue-lashing.

"Cheryl, please have a seat. I have been sitting here thinking what a disaster this may be for our company; however, I agree with Myles. He should be at his son's game," Darby said.

Myles couldn't believe what he just heard. Even worse, Cheryl was completely blown away with Darby's response. Her face had the look of someone who had just seen her very first boyfriend holding hands with someone else—complete shock. Both Cheryl and Myles sat quietly, not knowing what to say.

Darby stood and started to walk around the room. "I know that is a complete shock to both of you, but I have to tell you, Myles is right. I can't tell you the number of times in my life I wish I would have put my family ahead of my work. I didn't have balance in life for most of my married life. That is more than obvious since I am on my third marriage and my children have struggled finding their way in life. Myles is right. He is doing the right thing, Cheryl. I am going to support his decision, and I think you should, too." Darby walked over to Myles, shook his hand, and said, "I admire your courage. Now, let's figure out how to make this work."

"Sir, you did a great job in our meeting where we presented this idea. In fact, I was taken aback by your commitment and your presentation skills. I think you should consider doing the presentation. I can spend all the time you need between now and Thursday at five o'clock to bring you up to speed, coaching you through the presentation and everything we have prepared," Myles said as he watched Cheryl look on in amazement.

"I agree. I am comfortable doing the presentation. My only concern is how it looks to Vista Health to have the CEO doing the presentation. Does it make us look desperate, or does it show our commitment to getting this contract?" Darby half asked.

"Why don't you start with the famous Babe Ruth quote, 'Don't let the fear of striking out hold you back.' And then tell them that you wanted them to have every answer to every question they had right now, and since you are the decision-maker, you decided to come and do the presentation, despite the fears of some of the sales staff," Myles said. "I don't think it would hurt to tell them the truth. You supported your sales manager's decision to attend his son's championship basketball game tonight, so you agreed to do the presentation in his place so he could go to the game," Myles suggested.

Cheryl couldn't believe her ears. She just looked at both of them as they brainstormed, and it was obvious the decision was made. Darby was going to do the presentation.

CHAPTER 15

GAME DAY

J ake looked over his shoulder for what must have been the tenth time. He scanned the stands to see if his father was there. No sign of him. There were only two minutes left in the warm-ups, and he couldn't believe none of his family was there. Just then, he glanced at the door, and leading the way was his father, and behind him were his mom and two sisters. What he couldn't believe is they all had on matching orange T-shirts. Myles stopped long enough to pull the bottom of the shirt down as Jake looked. Myles's shirt said "Jake" in big letters, his mom's said "Go," his sister Emily's said "Fight," and his younger sister's said "Win." Jake couldn't believe it. He thought for a moment he might be embarrassed, and then he realized his dad was at his game in a personalized orange T-shirt for him. Jake beamed in pride and confidence. The gym was packed, and his dad and family were there to watch him.

The final score was 64 to 58; Jake's team had won!

After the game, Myles found Jake and gave him a huge dad-hug and said, "You did it! You won! You played great, Son! I wouldn't have missed this for the world!" Little did Jake know how true a statement that was.

Myles turned his phone off during the game and kept it off at the restaurant afterward for the celebration dinner. As they walked into the house, he turned it on to see if he had any messages about the meeting. Nothing. He decided he would not call tonight; he would just wait until the next day to see how it went. Myles thought to himself, *This is a moment I want to last the rest of the night! What a perfect day!* A call from work would only have shortened the experience.

Myles started for work early. Even Heather was anxious to push him out of the house and get him on his way to work. The whole office would be abuzz about the Vista. It was very unlikely a decision was made the previous night. Vista Health would probably want the weekend to think about the options, and then they would notify the winning company to start the documentation and contracting process.

"Good morning, Myles. Darby would like to see you in his office," Myles's admin said before he could put his stuff down.

"He is in early today," Myles replied.

"Um, I think he has been here a while. I am usually the first one here, and his light was on when I arrived," she replied.

Myles wondered where Cheryl was and if she wanted to tip him off on how it went before he walked into Darby's office. He noticed that her light was on, but she wasn't in her office. He went up to Darby's office.

"Myles, come in here," Darby said as he saw him approaching his admin.

"Sit down. Let's talk. How did the game go last night?" Darby said with a pursed smile.

"Great, they won sixty-four to fifty-eight, and Jake had a great game. In fact, he led the team in points and rebounds. It was a great game. We went out afterward for dinner to celebrate. It was great, thank you for asking," Myles replied.

"Well, it is over. I did the presentation last night, and it is over," Darby said with a downcast look.

Myles couldn't tell if "over" meant they completed the presentation. It almost sounded like "over" meant they had done poorly and Darby didn't feel like they were still in the running.

"So how did it go?" Myles asked.

Just then, Cheryl walked into the office and greeted Darby by saying, "Home run, Darby, complete home run!"

Myles looked around, and Cheryl had a huge smile on her face.

GAME DAY - 131

"You blew my surprise, Cheryl. I was just going to keep Myles on pins and needles," Darby replied, this time with a broad grin.

"Myles, you wouldn't believe how well it went. The short version is I think we won the story war. I don't just mean the battle; I believe we won the whole story war. The presentation was great. They loved our ArrowHead presentation, the clip of *Who's on First?* was a hit, and they commented on the fact that this was how they feel with some of their other software vendors. It went great," Darby said with complete enthusiasm. "We understood their business!"

"So what happened with the price issue?" Myles asked.

"It wasn't an issue. When we got to that point, I used the analogy of finding the best heart surgeon for saving the life of a loved one, and they agreed and didn't even hesitate at the price. In fact, after I discussed our pricing policy and the terms and conditions, the CFO said out loud, 'That falls within our range and is OK.' Oh, and at the very end, when we placed our keys on the table, the air in the room was palpable. Even their CFO chuckled and said both other finalists were late because they couldn't find their way to the Vista office," Darby said with a noticeable smile..

The pressure was off; Myles knew they felt good about the presentation. Whatever happened with the decision, he felt it couldn't be traced back to his decision to go to Jake's basketball game. Myles stood to congratulate everyone.

As he was leaving, Darby said, "Decision is today."

"Wow, that is quick. They aren't wasting anytime with this process," Myles replied.

"Sir, Vista Health is on line two," Darby's admin said as they were all standing and getting ready to leave.

Myles froze in his tracks. Cheryl looked at Darby and sat down in the chair in front of his desk. Darby slowly and calmly walked over to the phone, picked up the receiver, and said, "This is Darby."

There was an abnormally long pause in the conversation before Darby said anything. He nodded a few times and said the word "certainly." When Darby finally got the chance to speak, he said, "That will be fine. We can have our legal department have a draft of the contract to you by Tuesday. If you take a few days to review, we should be able to sign by next Friday, and we can start the implementation immediately. We will include a detailed implementation time line when we send the contract over for your review."

Both Cheryl and Myles looked at each other, and she silently high-fived Myles in a very uncharacteristic manner.

Darby ended the conversation, leaned back in his chair, and said, "Great day…this is a great day…simply a great day!"

Word spread quickly through the company. Everyone knew this was a big deal and a great team accomplishment. They also knew it was just the beginning of the real work, that of satisfying the customer and delivering more than they promised.

Myles sat at his desk and was about to pick up the phone to call Heather when he stopped and thought it would be fun to just send her a one-word text: *Paris!!!* It was less than thirty seconds later when he got the call from Heather.

"*Really*?" Heather said.

"Really," Myles replied. Myles gave Heather the play by play of what happened, and they agreed they would celebrate by making dinner reservations at the Bread Spot.

Myles hung up the phone and checked his computer. As he accessed his email, he was reminded that he never emailed Ted back after his last message. He felt badly about the time that had passed, and he clicked on reply.

Ted,

I cannot thank you enough for your last email. It came at a time when I needed the courage and commitment to follow through with my ArrowHead. You can rest assured you made a difference in my life.

I am sure you realize the effectiveness of your sales system and have seen it make a difference in your success. I am just now realizing, though, it isn't just about the sales system; the ArrowHead is more about life, the pursuit of meaningful happiness, and the quest for real purpose. I have spent the last few years of my life trying not to fail when I should have been pursing victory. It is never too late to change for the better. ArrowHeads successfully facilitate change. Ralph Waldo Emerson said, "It is not the length of life, but the depth." I believe I now understand that, thanks to you. Again, thank you is not enough. I look forward to your return so we can get together again for lunch or dinner, and this time, the treat is on me. Oh, and we need to get our families together in San Juan Capistrano; Heather is excited to meet you and your wife.

Thank you,

Myles

EPILOGUE

The summer passed very routinely. Ted and Myles continued to communicate, but they could never work their schedules out to meet in San Juan Capistrano.

Myles had obviously qualified for Pinnacle Club, and Paris was everything that Heather dreamed. She and Myles were able to stand on the top deck of the Eiffel Tower as the sun set and see the lights come on the tower and the city begin to light up.

Myles's father's health seemed to decline, and he was no longer as mobile, active, and healthy as before. In fact, Myles and Heather had some second thoughts about going to Paris, but at the urging of Myles's mother, they went ahead, and she agreed to watch the kids for the ten days while they were gone.

The Brickland Community Theatre hadn't solved their funding problem. The solution Myles worked toward only put a bandage on the real bleeding. He knew they needed more money, more of his time, and more work to ensure they could continue to provide a valuable cultural commitment to the community. In fact, Myles had committed to meet with the board of directors when he returned to determine if he or someone else should move the efforts ahead.

The real news was at the closing of the Paris Pinnacle Club retreat. As was typical, Darby usually gave a "State of the Company" speech to close the event. It was something everyone looked forward to because it was a wonderful rundown on what had happened, and more importantly, what was planned for the coming year. In addition, Darby always announced where the next Pinnacle Club event would be held for all the employees who qualified.

The entire group filled the room. Darby stood to start the speech. It was less than five minutes into the speech when he dropped the bombshell: "We have been approached by another company for acquisition. As you know, I have always rebuffed those opportunities. This time, however, their story and presentation was too compelling, and I listened. Tonight, I would like to announce that, as of last Wednesday, we have entered into a letter of intent to be purchased by AirTrek Technologies."

Myles didn't hear another word of the speech. Unbelievable. *What would this mean for everyone in the company?* He wondered. He looked to his phone just as he received a text message: *We need to talk, Ted.*

Authors

Kevan Kjar

Kevan Kjar founded ArrowHead3 Consulting to help companies with a complex product craft a story that resonates with their buyers, aligns their team, and helps them to deliver that story with passion. Kevan has worked with companies such as Siemens, Schlumberger, SAP, Oracle, Johnson & Johnson, HealthMedia and many others with strategic product initiatives on a repeat basis. He has assisted thousands of executive, sales and marketing professionals in countries around the world. Kevan began his sales career with WordPerfect Corporation in Washington DC serving clients such as the Supreme Court, Environmental Protection Agency, House of Representatives, Senate and other federal agencies. Kevan also has led marketing efforts at technology companies Manugistics and Baan. He holds a master's degree in Business Administration, and his hobbies include running marathons, hiking, traveling and collecting commercials. Kevan is a certified NLP practitioner and enjoys working with Boy Scouts and serving as a youth mentor. He and his wife Anita have five children and live in Boise, Idaho with their youngest son. *The ArrowHead: Winning the Story War* is his first book.

Kelly Shaw

Kelly Shaw has owned and operated over 15 separate companies and earned various awards as a business owner and entrepreneur. He has published a national newsletter on small business ownership and is the author of 3 books. He has continued to provide expert consulting services, and currently is providing merger/acquisition and business brokerage services for companies throughout the Northwest. He and his wife are the parents of 5 children and they have one grandchild. Kelly enjoys basketball, racquetball, golf, reading, carving, fly-fishing, gardening, and writing. He has traveled on business extensively throughout the U.S. He continues to volunteer at youth leadership camps and coaching youth sports teams.